HUMAN RIGHTS AND INDIGENOUS PEOPLES

A Handbook on the UN System

Florencia Roulet

IWGIA Document No. 92
Copenhagen 1999

HUMAN RIGHTS AND INDIGENOUS PEOPLES
A HANDBOOK ON THE UN SYSTEM

Copyright: Florencia Roulet and IWGIA

ISBN: 87-90730-07-0
ISSN: 0105-4503

Coordinators: Alejandro Parellada and Finn Kudsk

Translation from Spanish: Elaine Bolton

Cover and layout: Jorge Monrás

Print: Centraltrykkeriet Skive A/S
Skive, Denmark

*This book has been produced with
financial support from the European Commission*

**INTERNATIONAL WORK
GROUP FOR INDIGENOUS AFFAIRS**
Fiolstraede 10, DK 1171 - Copenhagen K, Denmark
Tel: (+45) 33 12 47 24 - Fax: (+45) 33 14 77 49
E-mail: iwgia@iwgia.org

About the author:

Florencia Roulet *is a graduate and teacher in history, with a post-graduate in international relations. She has lectured on American Ethno-History and Archaeology at the Faculty of Humanities (University of Buenos Aires) and has done research as fellow of CONICET (the National Council for Scientific and Technical Research, Argentina). In Geneva, she worked for the United Nations' Centre for Human Rights.*

She has published Guaraní resistance to the Spanish Conquest of Paraguay (1537-1556), *Posadas, Editorial Universitaria, in 1993. She has worked on the issue of the right of indigenous peoples to self-determination and is currently researching the history of treaties made between indigenous peoples and State authorities in Argentina and Chile.*

CONTENTS

Preface to the English Version 12

Introduction 16

Chapter 1:
Structure and function of the United Nations
with regard to human rights 22

A.-What is the United Nations? 22

*B.- The organs created by the Charter
of the United Nations* 23
    1 The General Assembly (GA) 23
    2 The Security Council (SC) 26
    3 The Economic and Social Council (ECOSOC) 27
    4 The Trusteeship Council (TC) 29
    5 The International Court of Justice (ICJ) 30
    6 The Secretariat 30

C.-The subsidiary organs 31
    1 From ECOSOC to the Working Group on
       Indigenous Populations 33
       a The Commission on Human Rights 33
       b The Sub-Commission on Prevention
          of Discrimination and the Protection of Minorities 35
       c The Working Group on Indigenous Populations 41
       d The Working Group on Contemporary Forms of Slavery 45
    2 The Commission on the Status of Women 47
    3 Technical Branches: the Office of the UN High
       Commissioner for Human Rights 48

Chapter 2
Submission of complaints to
the Commission on Human Rights 52

A.-The 1503 Procedure 52

B.-The 1235 Public Procedure 57

*C.-Specialized extra-conventional mechanisms
(Special Rapporteurs, Experts and Working Groups)* 59
    1   The Working Group on Enforced or
        Involuntary Disappearances 62
    2   The Special Rapporteur for Extrajudicial,
        Summary or Arbitrary Executions 64
    3   The Special Rapporteur on Torture 66
    4   The Working Group on the Arbitrary Deprival of Freedom 68
    5   The Special Rapporteur on the sale of children,
        child prostitution and child pornography 70
    6   Other specialized mechanisms of the Commission 71

Chapter 3
Submitting complaints to conventional bodies of the UN 74

A.-Introduction
    1   The international instruments 74
    2   The Treaty-monitoribg bodies 76
    3   The submission of individual complaints 78
    4   What can NGOs do? 79

B.-The International Bill of Human Rights 81

C.-Six international treaties on human rights 82
    1   The International Covenant on Civil and Political Rights;
        the Optional Protocol and the Human
        Rights Committee (CCPR) 82
    2   The International Covenant on Economic, Social and
        Cultural Rights and the Committee on Economic,
        Social and Cultural Rights (CESCR) 85
    3   The International Convention on the Elimination
        of All Forms of Racial Discrimination and the Committee
        on the Elimination of Racial Discrimination (CERD) 86
    4   The Convention on the Elimination of All Forms
        of Discrimination Against Women and
        the Committee on the Elimination of Discrimination
        Against Women (CEDAW) 88
    5   The Convention on the Rights of the Child and
        the Committee on the Rights of the Child (CRC) 90
    6   The Convention against Torture and
        the Committee against Torture (CAT) 93

*D.- Other international instruments of relevance
to indigenous peoples* 96

1 The Convention against Genocide and
     the International Criminal Court 96
  2 The Declaration on the Granting of Independence
     to Colonial Countries and Peoples and
     the Committee on Decolonization 100
  3 The Declaration on the Rights of People to Peace 101
  4 The Declaration on the Right to Development 101

Chapter 4
The specialized agencies of the UN
and indigenous peoples 104
  1 The International Labour Organization (ILO) 104
  2 The United Nations Educational, Scientific and
     Cultural Organization (UNESCO) 116
  3 The Food and Agriculture Organization (FAO) 122
  4 The World Health Organization (WHO) 123
  5 The World Bank 124
  6 The United Nations Development
     Programme (UNDP) 126
  7 The International Fund for Agricultural
     Development (IFAD) 127
  8 The World Intellectual Property
     Organization (WIPO) 128
  9 Other UN agencies of interest
     to indigenous peoples 129

Chapter 5
Bibliographic journey 132
  1 Fact Sheets of the UN Centre for Human Rights 132
  2 Human Rights Study Series 133
  3 Official documents of the United Nations 133
  4 A brief consultative bibliography on human
     rights and international organizations 140

Annexes

No. 1: Indigenous organizations which have
       consultative status with ECOSOC 142

No. 2: List of non-indigenous NGOs which
       may support indigenous causes and projects 144

No. 3: How to obtain consultative status with ECOSOC 149

No. 4: Draft Declaration of the United Nations
on the Rights of Indigenous Peoples,
approved by the WGIP in 1994 153

No. 5: Indigenous declarations regarding the
establishment of a permanent forum for
indigenous peoples within the United Nations 164

Index of key words 175

PREFACE

PREFACE

This Guide was originally conceived and written in Spanish and was aimed at a largely indigenous public from that part of the world which is commonly known as Latin America. The idea itself arose from direct contact with indigenous representatives from Latin America during meetings of the Working Group on Indigenous Populations in Geneva. Although at this level many of the representatives have a long and wide experience of international organizations, the subtleties of which they have come to know and understand intricately, many others feel incredibly disoriented when they first set foot in the bureaucratic labyrinth of the United Nations. This difficulty in identifying the competent organs and finding out what they do is largely due to a lack of available documents in Spanish explaining the complex structure of the UN in an accessible manner and helping to unravel the different possibilities which it offers.

On the other hand, there is an abundance of extremely good informational material in other languages, particularly in English, and this was very useful in the preparation of this Guide. Thus translating this text, which was published in 1997 in Spanish, into English has been a great challenge: it does not try to fill in gaps in information, nor does it aim to describe the way the UN human rights system operates more exhaustively than other available material. Its only desire is to collect basic information on the issue together into one organically designed text and to make that information accessible to readers - indigenous or not - so that they may follow through their inquiries themselves, as they wish.

The aim of this guide is to provide a collection of practical and up-to-date facts which will help indigenous users to benefit from the numerous UN human rights mechanisms. This will enable and encourage indigenous participation in the different international fora. Hopefully, it will also help to prevent violations of their human rights and to obtain compensation when this has occurred.

The great limitation of this kind of work is the impossibility of taking into account all the innovations and changes which, happily, are occurring in this area. Whilst it is incredible to note how much the international human rights machinery has grown and diversified over the last twenty years, the blazing progress of the "indigenous issue" within the United Nations is even more surprising. In 1982 the Working Group on Indigenous Populations was set up, a modest organ of the Sub-Commission on Prevention of Discrimination and Protection of Minorities. For more than a decade this was the only forum in the

United Nations to deal with indigenous issues. Today, its annual period of sessions brings together several hundred participants: representatives of States, of indigenous peoples and communities, observers from different agencies of the UN system, representatives from different NGOs sympathetic to indigenous causes, experts and other interested people. In its public meetings the problems, concerns and hopes of indigenous peoples around the world are discussed in complete openness, whilst the work of its members has brought about a large number of studies on issues of great importance as well as proposals to promote indigenous participation in decision making processes, both at a national and international level. An Open-ended Working Group of the Commission on Human Rights is currently considering and discussing the draft Declaration on the rights of indigenous peoples, whilst another Working Group will soon start reflections on the characteristics of a permanent forum for indigenous peoples within the UN system.

There are thus many inherent difficulties in updating the information contained in this Guide, fortunately made easier by the recent creation of the website for the United Nations High Commissioner for Human Rights, where an enormous number of documents can be consulted. In fact, the revision of the text, which was initially expected to be a mere adaptation of the content for an audience outside of Latin America, ended up with several chapters being rewritten in order to update and deepen the information provided. It is certain that a large part of this Guide will soon be out of date and omissions and errors will be inevitable. Nevertheless, we hope to bring some keys to the readers enabling them to complete this never ending task.

Florencia Roulet
October 1998

INTRODUCTION

INTRODUCTION

Information is power. It is an essential tool that enables you to get by in an increasingly complex world. It opens doors to those who possess it and closes them to those who have no access to it. For this reason, information has become a fundamental human right which all women, men and children of the planet should benefit from, without distinction.

For the effective defence of human rights in an international sphere, access to information is at the same time both essential and difficult to obtain, especially if you do not speak the diplomatic language of our time - English - and if legal vocabulary and the rules of the game of international organizations are foreign to you. Even if you manage to find out what mechanisms exist for the defence of human rights, you often do not know how to use them.

This guide was born from the desire to avoid such difficulties. It is aimed mainly at indigenous activists interested in defending the rights of their peoples and wishing to accompany and support their efforts. The starting point was the identification of the most serious and urgent problems which currently affect indigenous peoples. Situations such as genocide, ethnocide, racial discrimination, exploitation of labour, dispossession of land, forced displacement of people, extreme poverty, a lack of participation in political structures and in decision making are all part of the daily life of millions of indigenous people throughout the world. This Guide gives a detailed description of the international mechanisms which exist for the prevention and reparation of serious violations of these fundamental rights.

This book only covers the universal system for the protection and promotion of human rights (that is, the group of organs, procedures and mechanisms of the biggest international organization: the United Nations Organization), but it is important to be aware that many other useful mechanisms exist at a regional level, for example, within the framework of the Organization of American States (OAS). Due to lack of time and space this Guide does not cover regional mechanisms, but interested individuals and groups are advised to contact lawyers and NGOs experienced in the suitability of referring to them for each concrete case, because it may be that they are sometimes more effective than those of the UN.

For the majority of indigenous people around the world who have heard speak of it, the UN is a deep mystery: little or nothing is known of its aims, its structure, the relationships within it, its way of working and the results of its activities. This mystery creates great mistrust in many and a somewhat exaggerated level of expectation in others. For those with a greater knowledge of it, the UN tends to be an immense bureaucratic apparatus, closed in on itself, costly and unproductive, which nevertheless enables them to make use of a number of fora with a certain level of regularity and much unnecessary protocol where they make known their realities and set out their demands. Many wonder, with legitimate pessimism, what sense there is in the exhausting effort of approaching one of the organs to try to resolve problems. Indeed in spite of fifty years of existence, the UN is not only far from having fulfilled its objectives of maintaining international peace, encouraging friendship between countries, ensuring economic development and promoting respect for human rights, but is in fact a helpless observer to the explosion of tremendously violent conflicts, admits recognized dictators as Members, applies different criteria to reward or punish countries and during the last five decades has noted with indifference the growing inequalities between rich and poor nations.

All these doubts are valid. Nevertheless, in spite of its deficiencies, its slowness and its lack of autonomy in relation to the great political and economic powers of the world, the UNO does have many uses and this planet would probably be an even more violent, arbitrary and unjust place without it. In the field of human rights, although progress is slow and often difficult to perceive, there are developments worth mentioning: the conduct of States towards individual subjects under their jurisdiction, which until a few decades ago was considered a domestic issue, has gradually become a matter which is subject to the supervision of the international community. This is no small thing because often credit, investment, tourism and export markets, as well as the opportunity of being a part of the different international organizations, depend on the image of a country with respect to human rights. Although the UN is currently unable to punish States which violate human rights, the mere fact that one of its organs is investigating a situation in a country is a reason for that country to commit less abuses. This may not seem much, but each life saved, each person freed, each injustice avoided, justifies the existence of the UN.

This Guide aims to dispel the mystery around the nature of the UN, to reduce the mistrust of some and to curb the exaggerated enthusiasm of others by making available to readers a collection of basic information on the possibilities and limits for action of the United Nations in the area of human rights.

Chapter 1 describes the general structure of the United Nations and deals in particular with the political and technical organs which consider human rights issues. Chapter 2 explains a series of mechanisms for submitting complaints regarding human rights violations to organs created by the Commission on Human Rights and its Sub-Commission. In each case we try to analyse the effectiveness of these procedures and their limitations. Chapter 3 concentrates on the conventional mechanisms for submitting complaints, that is, the mechanisms established through international treaties ratified by the States. Chapter 4 deals with the specialized agencies of the UN which carry out activities of interest to indigenous peoples. Chapter 5, lastly, offers a bibliography to complete and update the information contained in this text. A series of Annexes provide useful information for indigenous activists who, either in Geneva or in their country of origin, are trying to make the most of the different mechanisms provided by the United Nations system.

How to use this Guide

This text is not intended to be a scholarly treatise but a brief and practical guide. Its aim is thus not to explain everything that exists on the issue of human rights within the universal system but to facilitate research and to direct the search for more complete information. It does not try to indicate which path to take, but to show that there are various directions possible and that it may be useful to try different paths.

The United Nation's organs and mechanisms for the protection of human rights are described as simply as possible, stressing the practical aspects and leaving out overly specific pieces of information such as the composition of each organ, the necessary requirements for the opening of sessions and decision taking (deliberatory and decisory quora), the type of majority required for a decision, the period of designation and the alternance of members, amongst other things. You should refer to the annexes or to other texts to supplement the information in this Guide. The UN's official publications are often given in brackets [] so that any person interested may find more information. For the same reason, a bibliography is included in the final chapter which will facilitate the search for other publications on the subject.

The Guide should not necessarily be read from beginning to end: the reader has the possibility of choosing the issues which interest him or her the most at any particular moment, according to his or her particular needs. Each chapter thus opens with a general explanation regarding the issue to be dealt with. Based on this introductory explanation, on the Index and the tables and diagrams, the reader can get a general overview of each theme and move on to specific questions. At the end of the Guide a list of the key words used in the text is included, indicating the page on which the definition of each term is to be found. Although each part of the Guide can be read separately from the rest, references to other chapters are also indicated throughout the text to avoid unnecessary repetition of information and to show the communication links which exist between the different organs and mechanisms devoted to human rights.

One final clarification: this Guide was written neither by indigenous people nor by lawyers. I am a history teacher and researcher who has dedicated myself for many years to issues related to the indigenous peoples of the American continent. Having worked as a volunteer, and later as a consultant, for the Centre for Human Rights between 1992 and 1994, I have been able to get to know the functioning of the complicated labyrinth of the United Nations from the inside. By reading, asking and interviewing the officials of the Centre, members of NGOs and human rights specialists, I have been able to unravel the information, which is here presented as a contribution to the commemoration of the International Decade for Indigenous Peoples.

I hope that this book will be useful to you, indigenous readers, that it will serve as a tool for opening doors and plotting the paths to be followed in a foreign environment. It is an environment which looks at you with surprise and sometimes with suspicion, but one which is at last beginning to see you, to recognise that you exist and to listen to your voices after more than five centuries of silence and oblivion.

March 1997

The writing of this Guide would not have been possible without the enthusiastic support of the World Council of Churches and the Dutch Episcopal Lenten Campaign (Vastenaktie-Nederland), which supported my project with enthusiasm and absolute generosity and which enabled me to carry it forward. This book sees the light of day thanks to the immediate interest with which the International Work Group for Indigenous Affairs (IWGIA) received the final text, generously assuming the arduous task of publishing and distributing it. I would like to express my deep thanks for the confidence that these organizations have shown in me and for the stimulus which they have given to my work.

Many people shared their time and valuable knowledge with me, helping me to achieve my task in one way or another. I would like to mention in particular the staff of the Centre for Human Rights, who invariably demonstrated their willingness to answer my questions and to provide practical information on the functioning of the UN's human rights system. My thanks to Daniel Atchebro, Fiona Blyth-Kubota, Julian Burger, Moctar Cisse, Luz Cuéllar, Kathryn Hinkle-Babul, David Johnson, Luca Lupoli, Francesca Marotta, Jacob Moller, Alexandre

Ovsiouk, Yanine Poc, Martha Rodríguez-Kaffer, Carmen Rueda Castañón and Myriam Tebourbi. A special mention must go to Miriam Zapata who pointed me in the right direction with regard to documentation, edited all the graphics and was constantly ready to cooperate with me in whatever way necessary, and to Manuela Tomei, of the ILO, who gave me her time and attention, providing me with all sorts of information.

Lastly, I would like to mention some good friends in Geneva who shared my enthusiasm for this project, who read, commented and enriched the text and who inspired me in my research; thanks to B. Giselda Fernándes, María Teresa Garrido and Liliana Valiña.

All of these people, and probably some whom I have forgotten to mention, were essential to the development of my work. To all of them, my sincere recognition for their valuable contribution. No omission or error which this Guide may contain are their responsibility.

Florencia Roulet

CHAPTER 1

STRUCTURE AND FUNCTION OF THE UNITED NATIONS WITH REGARD TO HUMAN RIGHTS

A. What is the United Nations?

As the Second World War came to an end, the victorious nations organized the San Francisco Conference, in which the **Charter of the United Nations** [DPI/511] was adopted. This document was the founding text of the United Nations Organization (UN), which was set up in October, 1945. Although the organization is known as the United "Nations", **only those countries recognized as sovereign States are included**. Thus the indigenous nations and peoples living within states are not represented in the UN. In December, 1945, the UN encompassed 51 Member States. By December, 1998, there were 185 Member States [*the complete list of member States of the UN can be consulted on the Internet at http://www.un.org/Overview/unmember.html*].

In order to gain a certain balance in the composition of its organs, different regions and political systems are represented within them. The UN currently recognizes five major regions of the world, using geographical and political criteria: Africa, Asia, Latin America, Western Europe and other States (including the United States, Canada, Australia and New Zealand) and Eastern Europe. Its **official languages** are **English**, **French**, **Russian**, **Spanish**, **Chinese** and, in some meetings, also **Arabic**.

The Charter of the United Nations (henceforward known as the Charter) establishes the overall principles of the organization and sets out its basic structure [*Preamble and Chapter 1*].

The founders of the United Nations were particularly concerned with the dramatic reality of war. For this reason, **the fundamental objectives** of the organization are:
- to maintain international peace and security;
- to develop friendly relations, respect, tolerance and cooperation between nations, based on respect for the principles of equal rights and the self-determination of peoples;
- to promote respect for human rights and fundamental freedoms, without distinction;
- to assure the economic and social progress of all peoples through international cooperation;
- to harmonize the actions of nations in the attainment of these common ends.

With regard to the structure of the UN, the Charter establishes six principal organs: the General Assembly, the Security Council, the Economic and Social Council, the Trusteeship Council, the International Court of Justice and the Secretariat. These bodies in turn can establish other organs to assist them on specific issues: **the subsidiary organs**. Some of these fulfil an extremely important role in the work the United Nations carries out with respect to human rights.

The UN furthermore has nineteen autonomous **specialized agencies**, which deal with a diverse number of issues (from health to meteorology, from culture to postal and telecommunications regulation). These include the World Health Organization (WHO), the International Labour Organization (ILO), the Food and Agriculture Organization (FAO), the International Monetary Fund (IMF) and the United Nations Educational, Scientific and Cultural Organization (UNESCO). All the organs of the United Nations, along with the specialized agencies, make up what is known as the **"United Nations system"**.

We will begin our tour of this system in a "horizontal" manner, presenting the six organs established by the Charter. We will then descend in a "vertical" manner through the subsidiary organs which deal with human rights issues, in order to see more clearly the UN structure and the place each organ occupies in the organizational hierarchy.

B. The Organs Created by the Charter of the United Nations

1) The General Assembly (GA)

Composition of the GA and participation in its deliberations:
Made up of representatives of all the Member States of the UN, the General Assembly is a sort of "parliament of nations" in which governmental views are reflected (this is why it is known as a **governmental organ**).

Apart from the Member States, which have both a voice and a vote in the General Assembly, some organizations may have **"observer status"** (which means they may participate in meetings of the General Assembly and other UN organs, but they are not permitted to vote).

There are four types of observers:
1) States which are not members of the United Nations (such as the Vatican and Switzerland);
2) national liberation movements (as was, for many years, the Palestine Liberation Organization or PLO, for example);
3) other intergovernmental organizations (such as the Organization of African Unity, OAU, the Organization of American States, OAS, etc.) and
4) the specialized agencies of the United Nations system.

> Only Member States and bodies with observer status may speak before the General Assembly, on invitation of the President of the Assembly.

- *Functions:*
- to deal with international cooperation to ensure maintenance of peace and security in the world;
- to initiate studies and make recommendations in order to:
  a) promote international cooperation in the political, economic, social, cultural, educational and health fields.
  b) to encourage the development and codification of international law (that is, to formulate Declarations, Covenants, Conventions and Protocols).
  c) to ensure the realization of the human rights and fundamental freedoms of all human beings, without distinction of any kind.
- to recommend means for the peaceful settlement of conflicts.
- others [*see Chapter IV, articles 9 to 22 of the Charter*].

As a "parliament of nations", **the General Assembly declares all new international standards formulated by its organs**. It also initiates studies on human rights issues (or requests them from its subsidiary organs), makes recommendations which have no binding commitment on the States and studies the recommendations of the Economic and Social Council.

> Since the proclamation of the Universal Declaration of Human Rights, the General Assembly has adopted more than sixty international instruments for promoting and protecting economic, social and cultural rights, political and civil rights, the rights of women, of children and of the mentally disabled, along with instruments which prohibit racial discrimination, genocide, slavery and apartheid, amongst other practices which infringe upon human dignity.

- *Period of sessions:*

The General Assembly holds one session per year in New York, between September and December, and may also hold an extraordinary session if the Security Council or a majority of the Member States request it.

- *How are decisions taken within the General Assembly?*

Through the principle of the sovereign equality of States, each Member State has a vote and decisions are taken by a two thirds majority of the

FUNCTIONS OF THE GENERAL ASSEMBLY AND ITS SIX COMMITTEES

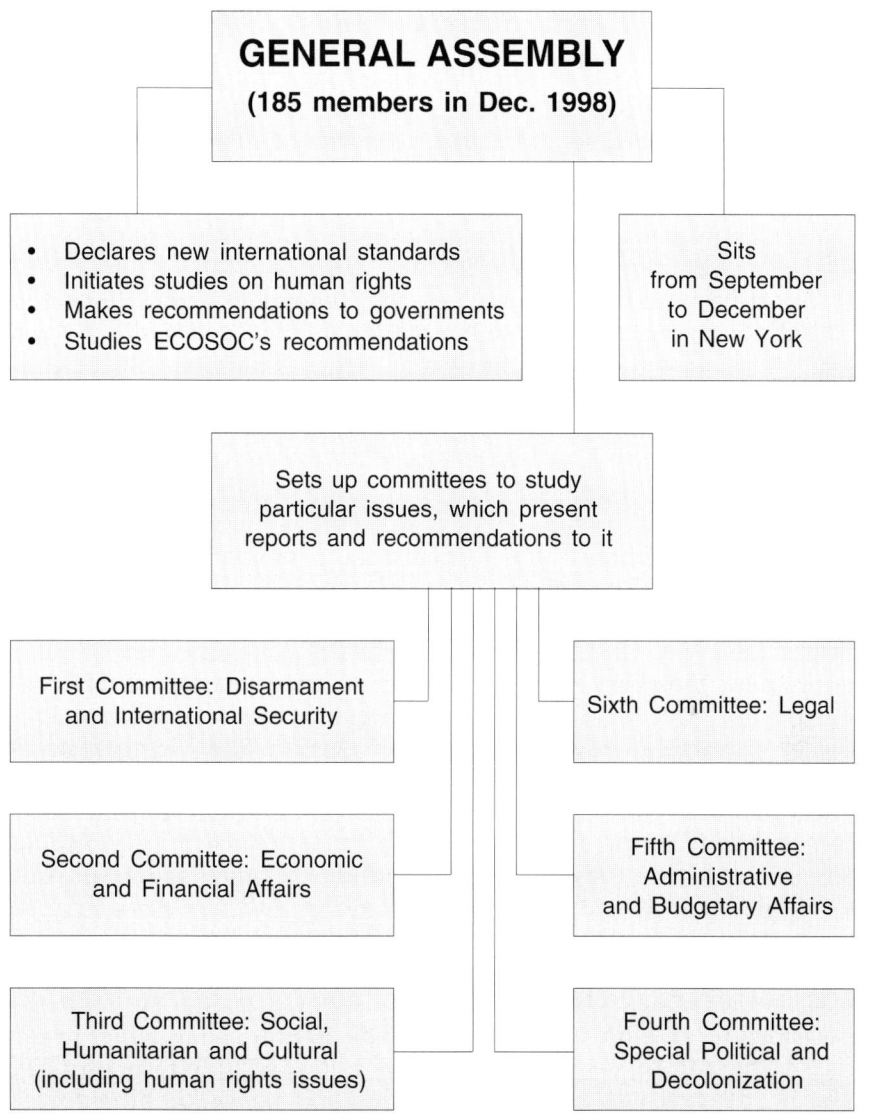

members present who have voted. These decisions are not legally binding, but a State may have recourse to the International Court of Justice to demand that they be respected. Theoretically, the United Nations can withdraw privileges from, and even expel from the organization, a country which repeatedly refuses to comply with decisions of the General Assembly, although this has never happened.

- *Subsidiary organs of the General Assembly*

The General Assembly has created a number of Committees to study specific issues and then submit reports and recommendations to the plenary Assembly. Generally, human rights issues are dealt with by the Third Committee, before being submitted to a plenary session of the General Assembly.

Apart from its main committees, the General Assembly has other subsidiary organs, such as the International Law Commission (which formulates proposals for international legal standards), the Special Committee on Decolonization, and others.

2) The Security Council (SC)

The Security Council's aim is to maintain international peace and security. It has 15 members, of which five are permanent (China, France, the Commonwealth of Independent States - Russia -, Great Britain and the United States of America) and another 10 non-permanent members, which rotate every two years. The SC promotes non-violent solutions to conflicts through negotiation, research, arbitration, mediation and conciliation. The Member States may submit any international conflict for its consideration and **its decisions are legally binding**. If they are not respected, the issue can be taken to the International Court of Justice, requesting an advisory opinion, or imposing economic or other **sanctions** (for example, an arms embargo). As a last resort, military force may be used against a country which refuses to obey its decisions although it has only opted to do this with certain countries (for example, Iraq) whilst other States which repeatedly disobey the Security Council's decisions receive no sanctions at all (this is the case of Israel in the face of numerous resolutions regarding the Occupied Territories). The SC also creates **observer missions** and **peace-keeping** forces (the "blue helmets"), in order to ensure fulfillment of cease-fires agreed between combatants.

> In order for a decision to be adopted by the Security Council, agreement on the part of all 5 permanent members is required, along with that of another 4 non-permanent members. Thus each permanent member has the **right of veto**, since if any one of them is opposed to a decision, that decision is blocked.

The SC sits permanently in session in New York and presents an annual report to the General Assembly. It can recommend the admission, suspension or expulsion of a Member State. It also makes recommendations to the General Assembly regarding candidates for each new Secretary-General and, together with the GA, appoints the judges to the International Court of Justice [*for more information, read chapters 5 to 8, articles 23 to 54 of the Charter and leaflet DPI/1005*].

3) The Economic and Social Council (ECOSOC)

- *Composition and periods of session:*

ECOSOC is made up of 54 representatives of the Member States, chosen by the General Assembly. It is thus also a **governmental organ**. It presents annual reports to the GA. It meets regularly twice per year (one organizational session in New York in February/March and one substantive session, from the end of June throughout July, which takes place alternately in New York and Geneva). It occasionally holds extraordinary sessions.

- *Functions:*

Apart from dealing with economic, social, cultural, educational and health issues, **ECOSOC must ensure respect for the human rights and fundamental freedoms** of all. In this respect, it makes recommendations, prepares draft conventions, organizes international conferences on human rights issues, sets up committees and coordinates activities with the specialized agencies, advising and recommending them. It also requests regular information from the specialized agencies and Member States on the measures adopted in order to fulfil its recommendations and gives an opinion on them.

- *Subsidiary organs of ECOSOC:*

There are two ECOSOC organs, both created in 1946, which deal directly with issues relating to human rights: the Commission on the Status of Women and the Commission on Human Rights. Other commissions which deal with issues of interest to indigenous people are the

Commission on Sustainable Development, the Commission on Transnational Corporations, the Commission for Social Development and the Commission on Narcotic Drugs.

ECOSOC also coordinates a series of **organs and programmes** which deal with social and economic questions, like for example, the Office of the United Nations High Commissioner for Refugees (UNHCR), the United Nations Children's Fund (UNICEF), the United Nations Conference on Trade and Development (UNCTAD), the United Nations Development Programme (UNDP), and the United Nations Environment Programme (UNEP). It also works with the specialized agencies *[the functions of ECOSOC are detailed in chapter 10, articles 61 to 72 of the Charter].*

- *ECOSOC and Non-Governmental Organizations (NGOs)*

ECOSOC has a Committee on Non-governmental Organizations (NGOs) which meets every two years to study requests from NGOs wishing to be recognized as consultative bodies in accordance with Resolution 1296 (XLIV) of 1968 *[Annex 6].* NGOs with consultative status may attend all public meetings of ECOSOC and its subsidiary organs.

> *What is consultative status with ECOSOC?*
> In accordance with the Charter, the Economic and Social Council may establish consultation mechanisms with non-governmental organizations (NGOs), as long as they are dealing with issues within its mandate. There are three types of "consultative status":
> - Category I (general consultative status): granted to NGOs concerned with most of the activities of ECOSOC;
> - Category II (special consultative status): granted to NGOs concerned with only a few of the activities covered by ECOSOC;
> - The Roster: a list of organizations that make occasional contributions useful to the work of ECOSOC or one of its subsidiary organs. NGOs with consultative status may make written and oral presentations to ECOSOC and its subsidiary organs.

NGOs with consultative status provide specialist, expert opinions to ECOSOC on issues which are being discussed. They reflect a wide sector of public opinion which may not necessarily be represented by their governments.

NGOs requesting consultative status must provide information to the NGO Committee regarding their aims to (which must be compatible

SUBSIDIARY ORGANS OF ECOSOC

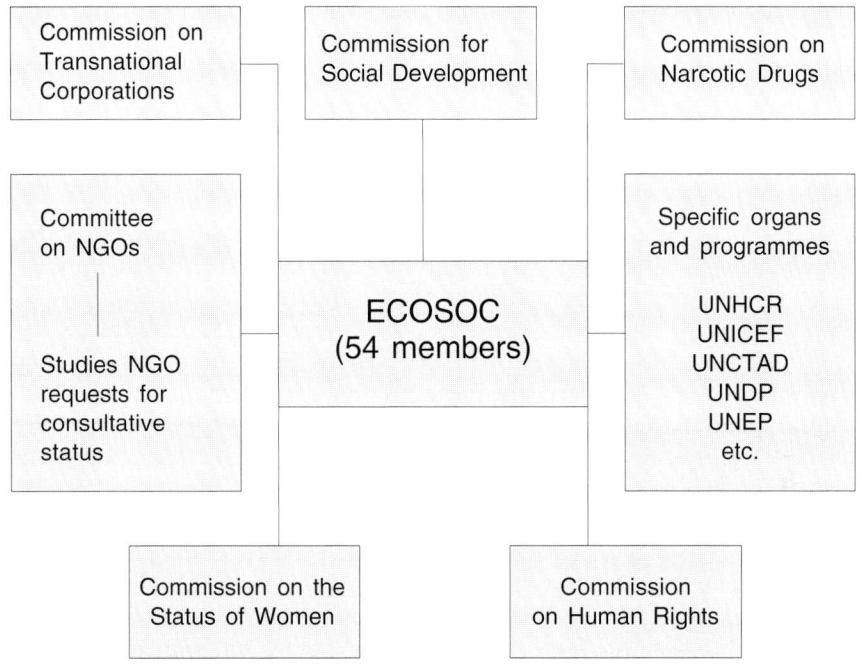

with those of the Charter), their work experience in the areas for which ECOSOC is responsible (development, human rights, environment, health, education, etc.), on recruitment of members and the funding sources on which they rely [see Annex No. 6]. The Committee then makes recommendations to ECOSOC regarding the candidate NGOs. Because of these requirements, the procedure for obtaining consultative status is slow and often takes several years.

4) The Trusteeship Council (TC)

The Trusteeship Council was set up to supervise the administration of colonial Territories under the protection of other Member States which had committed themselves to governing them and promoting the political, economic, social and educational advancement of their inhabitants. The administrating States were to lead these colonial territories progressively towards the development of self-government and independence. The TC initially dealt with 11 territories, 10 of which are today independent States. There currently remains only one Territory under supervision of the Council, the Pacific Islands, administered by the United States. This government presents an annual report to the TC [*see Chapters 12 and 13, articles 75 to 91 of the Charter*].

5) The International Court of Justice (ICJ)

This is the main legal organ of the UN and is based in The Hague (Netherlands). It is composed of 15 judges appointed by the GA and SC for a period of nine years, who act on a personal basis (that is, they are not representing their governments but are there on their own professional merit). There cannot be two judges from the same country.

The International Court of Justice **settles legal disputes** between States and gives **advisory opinions** on any legal issue presented to it by the General Assembly, Security Council or any other organ of the United Nations system authorized to do so by the GA. Member States are obliged to comply with the decisions of the ICJ on the following occasions: when the jurisdiction of the Court is recognized as legally binding, when it was agreed to submit the dispute in question to the Court or when treaties have been ratified which commit Member States to resolving their disputes in the Court [*for more information see Chapter 14, articles 92-96 of the Charter and the Statute of the International Court of Justice, within the same document*].

> Only States may submit conflicts to the International Court of Justice: indigenous peoples still have no direct access to it.

6) The Secretariat

Composed of the Secretary-General, who is the most senior official of the organization, and by the staff which he appoints, the Secretariat carries out a **secretarial role** in all the meetings of the United Nations organs and carries out all tasks delegated to it by those organs. Its activities and programmes are organized around five central themes: peace and security; economic and social affairs; development cooperation; humanitarian affairs and human rights. This last field of action is not a programme in its own right but is present and included within each of the previous four. The Secretary-General often assumes the role of supreme mediator in international conflicts and draws the attention of the Security Council to any issue which, in his opinion, is a threat to world peace and security. In recent years, actions aimed at building and consolidating peace following situations of conflict have gained increasing importance. In this sense, the Secretariat contributes to the development of conditions which encourage reconciliation, reconstruction and economic recovery. In order to achieve these objectives, its work includes the establishment and strengthening of national institutions, electoral supervision, reintegration and rehabilitation programmes for the victims of conflicts and the promotion of human rights.

Up until 1982, the Secretariat had a **Division of Human Rights** which provided services to all UN organs dealing with human rights issues. From 1982 until September 1997, this role was undertaken by the **Centre for Human Rights**, based in the United Nations Office in Geneva (Switzerland). The Office of the **UN High Commissioner for Human Rights** currently has responsibility for this area of work. We will look in more detail at the Office of the High Commissioner at the end of this chapter *[with regard to the Secretariat, see chapter 15, articles 97 to 101 of the Charter]*.

C. The Subsidiary Organs

We will now start to look at the organs which deal with human rights in a "vertical" direction. There first follows an explanation of the structure and functions of each one, and information on practical issues which those participating in their meetings should be aware of.

```
┌─────────────────────────────────────────────────────┐
│           ECONOMIC AND SOCIAL COUNCIL               │
│                     (ECOSOC)                        │
└─────────────────────────────────────────────────────┘
                          │
┌─────────────────────────────────────────────────────┐
│            COMMISSION ON HUMAN RIGHTS               │
│                   (Commission)                      │
└─────────────────────────────────────────────────────┘
                          │
┌─────────────────────────────────────────────────────┐
│   SUB-COMMISSION ON PREVENTION OF DISCRIMINATION    │
│             AND PROTECTION OF MINORITIES            │
│                  (Sub-Commission)                   │
└─────────────────────────────────────────────────────┘
                          │
┌─────────────────────────────────────────────────────┐
│        WORKING GROUP ON INDIGENOUS POPULATIONS      │
│                       (WGIP)                        │
└─────────────────────────────────────────────────────┘
```

To begin with, let us look at some important definitions:

What are human rights and fundamental freedoms?
These two concepts are complementary: **human rights** are those which, to be effectively achieved, need intervention on the part of the authorities: they must take steps to prevent, protect, secure, compensate or punish in order to ensure their fulfilment (for example, in the case of the right to housing, to work, to a fair trial, to health care, to non-discrimination). In contrast, **fundamental freedoms** are also rights but their fulfilment requires the non-intervention of the State, because this could interfere with their enjoyment (for example, freedom of conscience - the right of every person to think as he or she wishes -, freedom of religion, freedom of expression or assembly, etc.).

When we talk of human rights and fundamental freedoms we are including within these concepts an enormous number of rights, of both a **civil** nature (the right to life, liberty, a fair trial), a **political** nature (the right to participate in the political life of a country by voting or being elected) and a **social, economic and cultural** nature (the rights to individual and collective property, to work, to housing, to health care, to education, to meet peacefully, and to marry and have a family, amongst others).

All of these human rights are indivisible and interdependent: a person who freely enjoys civil and political rights but has no work, home, nor access to health care, for example, is the victim of human rights violations, just the same as a person arbitrarily deprived of his freedom or tortured. The rights of a minority are violated when people belonging to it are forced to abandon their language, religion or any other manifestation of their culture, just as the rights of workers are violated if they are not permitted to meet peacefully or to strike. **No category of human rights is more important than another:** the violation of any one is an offence to human dignity.

Human rights and fundamental freedoms have traditionally been considered as **individual rights** (of each human being, but not of groups). Now it is believed that some **essentially collective rights**, such as the right to peace, to development and to a clean environment, are also human rights. Many of the rights claimed by indigenous peoples are both individual and collective (above all, the right to land and its resources, to freedom from policies of genocide or ethnocide and the right to maintain the indigenous identity and culture of a group and its members). Thus the formulation of international legal standards for indigenous peoples requires a rethinking of many of the traditional concepts of human rights. For that reason, in order to highlight the specificity of their situation, many indigenous people prefer to talk of "indigenous rights " rather than of "human rights".

With these definitions in mind, we can now rapidly look at the main United Nations organs which deal with human rights.

1) From ECOSOC to the Working Group on Indigenous Populations

a) The Commission on Human Rights

The Commission on Human Rights is one of the six commissions established by ECOSOC in 1946, henceforward known as "the Commission".

- *Composition and periods of session:*

The Commission is a **governmental organ**, because it incorporates representatives of 53 Member States chosen by ECOSOC, for a three-year term. It meets for six weeks every year in March and April, in Geneva.

> In the Commission's meetings, only the 53 Member States or their alternates have the right to vote, but other Member States of the UN, the organizations with observer status and the non-governmental organizations (NGOs) who have consultative status with ECOSOC, are permitted to speak.

- *Functions:*

The Commission undertakes a variety of different tasks, which are all, however, closely linked. One is the **promotion of human rights**. This consists of identifying problems, highlighting insufficiencies in national legislation or establishing that violations have taken place, in order to search for and propose solutions to prevent such situations from occurring again in the future. This is essentially a preventive role, which is achieved through the preparation of studies, research and reports and the formulation of international standards. Its second task is that of the **protection of human rights**, which tends more towards ensuring that States strictly respect the human rights laid out in existing international standards and that proven violations are punished.

- *What does the Commission do to protect human rights?*

The Commission is not a Court of Law and cannot sanction States, but over the last few years it has established specific **procedures** for supervising the human rights situation within the different countries and for investigating complaints of human rights violations. On the one hand, there are a number of mechanisms for studying important human rights issues (be they specific themes, such as torture or enforced disappearances; or be they countries in which the human rights situation is particularly serious, such as Chile under the Pinochet dictatorship, Guatemala or Haiti, to name but a few). These mechanisms may be the responsibility of a group of individuals (generally five experts, one for each major geographical region of the world), in which case it is known as a **Working Group**, or of one person, known as an **Expert or Special Rapporteur** *[see specialized mechanisms in Chapter 2].*

On the other hand, the Commission has a procedure for the presentation of individual complaints (or **"communications"**) regarding **systematic and large scale violations of human rights** (that is, violations being perpetrated regularly, with the same methods and affecting a large number of people). This mechanism, established in 1970 by ECOSOC Resolution 1503 is now better known as the "1503 Procedure" *[see Chapter 2].*

How does the Commission on Human Rights function?

OBJECTIVE	ACTIVITIES
The promotion of human rights (preventive role)	It prepares • Studies • Reports • Proposals for international standards (Declarations, Covenants and Conventions on human rights). It coordinates human rights activities within the United Nations system.
The protection of human rights (corrective role)	It appoints Special Rapporteurs, Experts and Working Groups to study particular issues and investigate complaints: specialized mechanisms. It receives individual complaints regarding massive and systematic human rights violations: the 1503 Procedure.

b) The Sub-Commission on Prevention of Discrimination and Protection of Minorities (Sub-Commission)

- *Composition and period of sessions:*

Set up in 1947, the Sub-Commission is the principal subsidiary organ of the Commission. It has 26 members, chosen by the Commission for a four-year term of office. The members of the Sub-Commission are independent experts, proposed by their respective governments but there on personal merit and not representing their country's authorities. Thus it can be said that the Sub-Commission is a **non-governmental organ** of the United Nations.

It meets annually, for a period of four weeks in August, in Geneva. Apart from its members (or alternates), observers from governments, national liberation movements, other United Nations organs, specialized agencies, intergovernmental organizations and NGOs in consultative status with ECOSOC have the right to participate in the meeting.

- *Functions:*

The Sub-Commission can initiate studies on the **prevention** of whatever type of discrimination which is contrary to human rights. It can also study possible measures for the **protection** of racial, national, religious and linguistic minorities. On the basis of these studies, it must make recommendations to the Commission. The Sub-Commission may also carry out any other role assigned to it by ECOSOC or the Commission.

In order to take forward studies on new issues and problems relating to human rights, a number of its members are nominated as Special Rapporteur. The role of Rapporteur terminates once the study is finished. With regard to indigenous peoples, in 1993 Dr. Erica-Irene Daes completed her "Study on the Protection of the Cultural and Intellectual Property of Indigenous Peoples" and in 1995 her "Draft Principles and Guidelines for the Protection of the Heritage of Indigenous Peoples". Since 1997 she has been working on a study of the relationship between indigenous peoples and their lands. Dr Miguel Alfonso has finished a "Study on Treaties, Agreements and other Constructive Arrangements between States and Indigenous Populations", which he has been working on since 1989 *[see Bibliography for codes of the published reports]*.

- *Subsidiary organs of the Sub-Commission:*

Given that **the Sub-Commission's work is primarily that of the study of human rights issues**, its subsidiary organs do not have the authority to deal with complaints of human rights violations, except in the Working Group on Communications, which studies complaints lodged under the 1503 Procedure *[see Chapter 2]*.

The Sub-Commission currently has three Working Groups which meet in the weeks prior to its annual session in August (they are thus known as the "pre-sessional Working Groups"):

1) the Working Group on Communications, which studies complaints lodged under the 1503 Procedure, selects those which seem to be the most proven and submits them for the Sub-Commission's consideration *[see Chapter 2]*;

2) the Working Group on Contemporary Forms of Slavery, which looks into all practices related to slavery and the treatment of slaves *[see further on, point d]*;

3) the Working Group on Indigenous Populations *[see point c]*.

MANDATE RECEIVED	ACTIVITIES UNDERTAKEN
• To initiate studies on new issues and concerning human rights problems	• Designation of Special Rapporteurs (SR)
• To prepare draft international standards (Declarations, Covenants, Conventions)	• Creation of thematic Working Groups (WG) to draw up drafts. Confidential meeting of the Working Group on Communications
• To make recommendations to the Commission on Human Rights	• Inclusion of recommendations and draft for resolutions in the annual report, on the basis of proposals made by the SR and the WG

A number of other Working Groups meet during the sessional period in August. In general, they are limited to achieving a specific task (such as preparing a draft declaration or convention or suggesting improvements in the working methods of the Sub-Commission, for example), and once their work is finished they are dissolved.

Some practical issues relating to NGO participation in meetings of the Commission on Human Rights and its Sub-Commission:

- The Commission and Sub-Commission organize their work in accordance with the **Rules** of Procedure of the Functional Commissions of the Economic and Social Council [*Doc. E/5975/Rev.1. Sales NE S.83.I.10*]. This is a useful document to read carefully in order to understand the regulations governing the functioning of these two bodies.

- Only NGOs in consultative status with ECOSOC may **present written documents or speak** during these meetings. Many of these NGOs are willing to provide speaking time to others who do not have consultative status, if the issue being discussed falls within their field of expertise. It is thus extremely important to work in close contact with NGOs which are accredited with ECOSOC, both indigenous and non-indigenous [*see list of NGOs in Annexes 1 and 2*].

- **Written interventions** may be made regarding any item on the agenda. The text must be short (not more than 2,000 words), well written and containing information relevant to the issue under discussion, which has been obtained from reliable sources. These texts are translated into all the official languages of the United Nations as meeting documents. If an NGO wishes to make a written presentation, it must be sent to the Office of the UN High Commissioner for Human Rights at least six weeks prior to commencement of the period of session.

- In order to participate in the session, each delegate must **be "accredited"** with the NGO Liaison Office. It is best to commence this process prior to travelling to Geneva: the most senior member of the NGO with consultative status to which the delegate belongs (or which is supporting the delegate) must write a letter one month before commencement of the meeting, nominating the representatives to travel to Geneva and requesting the necessary documentation for each one. The security guards controlling access to the Palais des Nations will allow nobody in without the necessary documentation and thus each delegate must bring a copy of this letter and proof of identity in order to obtain entry on the first day until he or she has received the necessary pass.

- At the end of each session of the Commission or Sub-Commission, a **provisional agenda** is approved for the subsequent session, and this is published at the end of the report. This agenda is drawn up on the basis of existing mandates which are renewed on a yearly basis, on new issues proposed in each session and on urgent issues which arise during sessions. In order to propose a new item for the agenda, the NGO must obtain the agreement of a member (a government in the case of the Commission, or an expert in the case of the Sub-Commission) to present the proposal for them. Appropriate documentation must be provided to the Secretariat for each item on the agenda.

- On the first day of the session, a President is elected and a Bureau is set up comprised of the President, three Vice-Presidents and a Rapporteur. This Bureau goes through the provisional agenda and proposes the **final agenda**, including the amount of time to be spent on each item. Last minute amendments are always made to this agenda, above all in the last weeks of the meeting. At the beginning and end of each day, the President announces any changes to the agenda, which resolutions are to be voted on and which Working Groups are going to meet. Delegates willing to speak to only on one or two precise items on the agenda only must therefore be in frequent contact with the Office of the UN High Commissioner for Human Rights in order to plan their trip accordingly.

- Those participating in meetings of the Commission and Sub-Commission require a large amount of **documentation** (provisional agenda, report from the previous session, reports and studies from the special rapporteurs and working groups, written interventions to be presented by governments, specialized agencies and NGOs, list of participants, etc.) These papers are available at no cost from the Documentation counter (second floor, on the left of door 40), by presenting your pass and the exact code of each document. Only one copy per accredited delegate is allowed. Documents of a more general nature can also be obtained here, such as fact sheets, copies of international instruments, a timetable of UN conferences and meetings, etc. Not all these documents are provided free of charge and so you must have ready the Sales Number and sufficient money to pay for them.

- For each item on the agenda, the Secretariat prepares a **list of speakers**. Each list is generally opened two days before the item is to be discussed and closes once the discussion is underway: you need to be well aware of when the registration period is! (the President of the Bureau announces it in advance). NGOs with consultative status have the right to speak once only on each item on the agenda. If you know which items you wish to speak on before travelling, you can register on the list by writing to the Office of the UN High Commissioner for Human Rights before the period of session. In accordance with the rules of procedure, the list of speakers is organized in the following way: firstly, members of the Commission or Sub-Commission, followed by representatives of Member States, observer States and liberation movements recognized by the GA, then representatives of other UN organs and its specialized agencies and finally NGOs, in order of registration.

- The Bureau only accepts **contributions** which are directly relevant to the topic under discussion and rejects politically motivated speeches or those which involve aggressive or insulting language. It is necessary to be careful when deciding which agenda item you wish to speak on and to prepare each speech, so that you do not run the risk of losing your right to speak. Indigenous representatives attending the meetings of the Sub-Commission tend to intervene in items 6 ("Violation of human rights and fundamental freedoms...") and 15 ("Discrimination against indigenous peoples"), but there are other items on which it would be possible to intervene: item 4 ("Discussion of new events..."), 5 ("Elimination of racial discrimination"), 7 ("the New International Economic Order and the promotion of human rights") and 8 ("Achieving economic, social and cultural rights"). In the Commission, apart from item 12 ("Violation of human rights...") and 17 ("Sub-Commission's Report"), there has also been, since 1996, an item 23 ("Indigenous Affairs").

- In order to **prepare a speech**, it is useful to ask the help of an experienced NGO. An objective and dispassionate language must be used, avoiding criticism of any particular government (unless the agenda item includes a study of the human rights policies of that particular government) and should include constructive suggestions rather than just complaints and criticisms. If an NGO considers it particularly important to name a country, it could organize its presentation around a general issue (for example, enforced disappearances, racial discrimination or population displacements) and give a number of examples to illustrate what it is saying, if possible mentioning cases which have occurred in a number of different countries.

- Oral presentations should last between **five and ten minutes**. There is simultaneous translation into other languages. It is important to speak slowly and clearly so that the interpreters can do a good job and everyone can understand what is being said. It is preferable to have a written text and to make sure that each interpreter receives a copy before commencing the speech: this helps them greatly. The Secretariat and observers in the Chamber also want copies of each speech and they generally request them from the speaker when he or she has finished speaking. It is worth having between 15 and 20 copies ready. If the NGO refers to the situation in a particular country, it is usual to give the representative of that State a copy of the speech just before making it, so that they can follow attentively and prepare their reply.

- **Both the benefits and risks of presentations** to the Commission and Sub-Commission must be weighed up: these presentations are public and the rules are not as strict as the normal mechanisms for making complaints. Because of this, they have a much greater impact and a more rapid effect than the procedures we will be analyzing in the coming chapters. However, this method has to be used responsibly: a false accusation based on insufficient grounds or presented in an overly politicized or aggressive language and tone could greatly damage the reputation of the NGO making it. Furthermore, in countries with repressive regimes, human rights activists and their families put themselves in great danger by daring to denounce publicly their governments. In these cases, it is sometimes more sensible to use the confidential mechanisms thus exposing these people and their families less.

- For a **Resolution** to be approved on one or more issue of interest, it is not sufficient to speak before the Commission or the Sub-Commission on the relevant point on the agenda. Only members of these two organs can present motions for Resolutions. A Resolution is an action agreed and adopted by a political organ (the Sub-Commission, Commission, ECOSOC or the General Assembly). Although their effect is moderate, as they are often not fulfilled, Resolutions are essential in order to put into practice a **decision** of these organs (nominate a Special Rapporteur, organize a conference, create a new body, order an investigation, etc.) To promote a motion for a Resolution, it is necessary for a Member State of the Commission or an expert member of the Sub-Commission to present it and push for other members, as well as governmental representatives and NGOs, to support it. Some NGOs start circulating draft resolutions from the first week of the meeting, to be sure of getting the necessary support.

- The meetings of the Commission and the Sub-Commission are not only important for what is said and decided in plenary, but also for all the **contacts** that are made in the bars and corridors. Delegates have the possibility of conversing informally with members of the Commission or Sub-Commission over a number of weeks, thus providing them with up-to-date information, telling them about their work and proposing resolutions. It is often useful to get to know the government representatives (especially those from your own country or region) and to get on good terms with them. This helps to build trust and sometimes enables support to be gained. Lastly, contacts between NGOs are extremely important in order to be able to work in a consolidated and coordinated fashion in the future. This lobbying is one of the most important activities of these sessions.

- The Commission's **report** is generally ready to be submitted to ECOSOC in July. The Sub-Commission's report is available in October or November of each year. Reports can be requested from the United Nations Documentation Centres in various countries *[see list and addresses in Annex 5]*. As from 1998, many reports can be directly accessed via the Internet site of the Office of the UN High Commissioner for Human Rights: http://www.unhchr.ch.

c) The Working Group on Indigenous Populations (WGIP)

- *Composition and period of sessions:*

This Working Group, made up of five independent expert members of the Sub-Commission, meets annually in Geneva for one week at the end of July or beginning of August. **Its meetings are public** and government observers, UN specialized agencies, NGOs with or without consultative status, and in fact any organization, people or indigenous community that wishes to can attend. This flexibility with regard to participation on the part of indigenous organizations, as well as academics and experts interested in the subject, has meant the WGIP has become one of the most lively and popular meetings of all those organized by the UN in the field of human rights *[see Fact Sheet No 9 Rev. 1: "The Rights of Indigenous Peoples"]*.

- *Functions and activities of the WGIP:*

The Working Group on Indigenous Populations was established in 1982 with two **mandates**: 1) **to study events** which, on a national, regional or world level are related to the human rights and fundamental freedoms of indigenous peoples and 2) **to formulate new international standards** regarding the rights of these peoples. The Working Group prepares a report which is submitted annually to the Sub-Commission, presenting its conclusions and recommendations. The Sub-Commission then passes this report on to the Commission, along with its own.

In line with the first mandate, the members of the Working Group receive information from governments, intergovernmental organizations, the specialized agencies of the UN and NGOs on social, economic, legal and political developments in the situation of indigenous peoples throughout the world. Although NGOs often present proof of serious violations of the human rights of a number of different indigenous peoples, **the Working Group is not a body with the authority to receive and investigate complaints, nor to make recommendations to governments**. Nevertheless, for the WGIP, well-founded complaints are a source of information regarding the reality of indigenous peoples and the problems they are faced with. With this information, its members are in a better position to fulfil their second mandate, the formulation of standards.

In this respect, the Working Group worked from 1985 to 1993 on a **draft Declaration of the Rights of Indigenous Peoples**. The first version was a text containing seven "basic principles" *[see Annex II of the WGIP report in document E/CN.4/Sub.2/1985/22]*. In July 1993, the five members of the WGIP approved the final version of the draft, which consists of 45 articles *[see Annex 7]*. This draft Declaration was unanimously approved by the Sub-Commission and now has to be studied, discussed and approved, or possibly amended, by the other superior organs: the Commission, ECOSOC, the Third Committee of the GA, and a plenary session of the General Assembly before the end of the International Decade of the World's Indigenous Peoples (December, 2004). In 1995 the Commission decided to create an open-ended Working Group which would meet in the periods between sessions with the aim of formulating a draft declaration on the basis of what was drafted by the WGIP and approved by the Sub-Commission.

> Apart from the monitoring of human rights situations and the formulation of standards, the WGIP has encouraged and initiated a number of basic **studies** on subjects relevant to indigenous peoples (the intellectual and cultural property of indigenous peoples, treaties and agreements between indigenous peoples and States, multinational activity on indigenous lands) and has organized international **conferences and seminars** to discuss these and other issues (environment and sustainable development, self-government, racism and racial discrimination in economic relations, land).

Although the drawing up of the draft Declaration is now at an end, the Working Group continues to have a great deal to do: analyzing developments in events affecting the rights and freedoms of indigenous peoples; commencing new studies on relevant issues; consulting with governments, intergovernmental organizations and NGOs in order to present proposals on the International **Decade of the World's Indigenous Peoples** (December, 1994-December, 2004), and considering the role a **Permanent Forum** for Indigenous People could play within the United Nations system. In 1997 it was decided to address the issue of the formulation of guidelines or codes of conduct for mining and energy producing companies in the private sector. It could possibly also begin work on an International Convention on the Rights of Indigenous Peoples.

- *New temporary organs set up by the Commission on Human Rights*

In 1995, the Commission on Human Rights decided to create an **open-ended Working Group to formulate a draft Declaration** on the basis of the WGIP's draft which was approved by the Sub-Commission in 1994 [*Annex No. 7*]. Any Member State of the Commission, along with those indigenous organizations which have been approved by ECOSOC's NGO Committee may take part. The procedure established by the Commission for the participation of indigenous organizations which do not have consultative status with ECOSOC is detailed in the Annex to Resolution 1995/32 of the Commission on Human Rights. The first meeting of this Working Group took place in 1995, in Geneva [*see the relevant report in E/CN.4/1996/84*]. In its third period of session (October, 1997), the Working Group adopted two articles of the draft Declaration at first reading.

It is the General Assembly who must approve the final text and proclaim the United Nations Declaration of the Rights of Indigenous Peoples. Consequently, **the Declaration still has no legal status** and it could take several years before it is proclaimed by the General Assembly (in theory, the GA should adopt the Declaration during the International Decade of the World's Indigenous Peoples).

In 1993, the World Conference on Human Rights in Vienna requested that the General Assembly consider the **creation of a permanent forum** for indigenous peoples within the UN system during the International Decade [*A/CONF. 17/23, p. 20*]. This recommendation gave new momentum to the reflection and debates on the issue, which had already been raised by indigenous organizations in the 1980s at the Working Group on Indigenous Populations. Firstly, the General Assembly asked the Secretary-General to draw up a document examining the existing mechanisms, procedures and programmes of the United Nations with regard to indigenous peoples [*A/51/493*]. Secondly, the governments of Denmark (in association with the Greenland Home Rule Government) and Chile both sponsored seminars (Copenhagen, 1995 and Santiago de Chile, 1997) to discuss proposals for a possible permanent forum [*the reports of these seminars are found in documents E/CN.4/Sub/2/AC/4/1995/7 and and Add. 1 to 3 and E/CN.4/1998/11, Adds. 1 and 2 respectively*]. At the same time, the indigenous organizations themselves felt the need to meet together to develop a common strategy and to present unified proposals to the different authorities who were studying the issue. This gave rise to the Regional Conferences of Temuco (Chile) in 1997 and Ukepseni (Panama) in 1998, where issues such as the hierarchical level which the permanent forum should occupy, the breadth of its mandate and indigenous participation in its structure as well as its relations with the Working Group on Indigenous Populations were discussed *[the declarations from both Conferences can be found in Annex 8].*

In the light of this, in March, 1998 the Commission on Human Rights decided to create a new open-ended Working Group, to meet between sessions, with the aim of drawing up and examining proposals for the establishment of a permanent forum. Indigenous participation in this Working Group will be according to the same criteria which govern the Working Group which is drawing up the Declaration *[see above].*

The main task of the Working Group on the permanent forum will be to define the mandate of this new organ, its position within the United Nations system (which organ it will report to and thus what its place in the hierarchy will be), its composition (in particular, how indigenous peoples will be represented within it), its rules of operation and its financing. The Working Group must submit its report to the Commission in 1999.

- *What is the Voluntary Fund for Indigenous Populations?*

To encourage participation of as many indigenous delegates as possible in the WGIP meetings, a United Nations Voluntary Fund for Indigenous Populations was set up in 1985. This fund receives donations from governments, NGOs and individuals and with the money collected assists indigenous delegates with the costs of visiting Geneva. If delegates decide to stay on in Geneva for meetings of the Sub-Commission or for other reasons, the Fund does not cover these additional costs. Since 1996, the Voluntary Fund has also provided resources for meetings of the **Commission's open-ended Working Group** to draw up a Declaration of the Rights of Indigenous Peoples. In this case, only indigenous organizations with the prior approval of ECOSOC's NGO Committee may apply for funding from the Board of Trustees of the Voluntary Fund.

Indigenous organizations wishing to request financial support from the Voluntary Fund should send this information to the Office of the UN High Commissioner for Human Rights by 30th March each year *[there is a detailed questionnaire annexed to Fact Sheet No 9 Rev. 1]*. **The Board of Trustees of the Voluntary Fund** meets in Geneva in May to study requests and, according to the resources available, to decide which applications to support. This Board of Trustees is largely made up of indigenous people from around the world.

> *What information is requested to apply for financial assistance from the Voluntary Fund?*
>
> 1) The full name of the indigenous organization or community to which the candidate or candidates belong.
>
> 2) A short description of their role in the organization or community.
>
> 3) The name of the indigenous people (or indigenous peoples) which the organization represents or to which the community belongs.
>
> 4) The costs to be covered by the Voluntary Fund (flight only; travel and costs of stay) and the itinerary (for example, Guatemala City - Geneva - Guatemala City). The Voluntary Fund always pays the shortest distance between the candidate's place of residence and Geneva.
>
> 5) Information on the candidate or candidates: full name, background and experience in indigenous affairs, home address, languages spoken (including indigenous languages).
>
> 6) A brief description of the theme or themes that each delegate will cover in his or her presentation to the Working Group.

d) The Working Group on Contemporary Forms of Slavery

- *What it does, where and when it functions:*

This Working Group of the Sub-Commission was set up in 1974. It meets once per year in Geneva, for a period of 8 days, in May.

Apart from **receiving information** on traditional forms of slavery (in which the slave is the property of another person, and is bought and sold as a marketable product), this Working Group **studies a number of contemporary practices**, generally clandestine, which are also considered as forms of slavery: debt servitude; child trafficking; child labour and the use of children as soldiers in armed conflicts; child pornography; female child genital mutilation; the traffic of individuals for use as prostitutes; street children; racial segregation and colonialism.

The meetings of the Working Group are open and participation on the part of governmental observers and NGOs (with or without ECOSOC consultative status) is welcomed.

- *How it works:*

The WG is authorized to **examine events** related to slavery, to consider and **study** all **information** received from credible sources and to **recommend corrective action**. Some governments provide information on the measures they have taken to implement the three existing Conventions on Slavery: the 1926 International Slavery Convention, the 1956 Supplementary Convention on the Abolition of Slavery and the 1949 Convention on the Suppression of the Traffic in Persons and of the Exploitation of the Prostitution of Others, but it is not a supervisory organ of these international treaties. In fact, very few governments participate in its discussions (generally no more than fifteen). It also receives information from various NGOs, above all Antislavery International, Terre des Hommes, Defence for Children International and the International Abolitionist Federation.

> This WG chooses a special theme each year which it studies and on which it formulates national and international action programmes, recommending measures to be adopted. It also organizes seminars and study days and supports the drafting of a Convention on inter-country child adoption.

The Working Group on Contemporary Forms of Slavery has **no established mechanism for lodging complaints**, although its members sometimes receive communications from the Secretariat.

There is a **Voluntary Fund for Contemporary Forms of Slavery**, which was originally created in order to contribute to the costs of travel and stay in Geneva for NGO representatives who wanted to provide information to the WG. It is now being considered for use in the financing of rehabilitation and compensation projects for victims of slavery and their families (following the example of the Voluntary fund for Victims of Torture). The fund is currently a very small one.

To send or request information from the Secretariat of the WG on Contemporary Forms of Slavery, the telephone number is (4122) 917-9330; the fax number is (4122) 917-9010.

> People (victims and families) and interested NGOs should send requests by the end of January to the Office of the UN High Commissioner for Human Rights, addressed to the Voluntary Fund for Contemporary Forms of Slavery. This must include name, occupation (in the case of an NGO, status and sectoral and regional areas of operation), a reliable contact address, a description of the project and an indication of who will be the beneficiaries. All requests must mention the amount of funding requested and for what purpose it will be used. NGOs must indicate their annual budget and their funding sources. There is a questionnaire for requesting funds from the Voluntary Fund.

2) The Commission on the Status of Women

This Commission is also a subsidiary organ of ECOSOC and makes recommendations to improve the status of women socially, politically, legally and economically with the aim of achieving equality of rights between men and women.

It is a **governmental organ** composed of 45 members which deals with the **formulation of standards** (it draws up international instruments such as the Convention on the Elimination of Discrimination against Women) and **to supervise the application** of some of these standards. Furthermore, this Commission prepares International Conferences on Women (such as the Beijing Conference of 1995) and adopts resolutions and decisions which must be subsequently approved by ECOSOC.

The Commission on the Status of Women meets every year in Vienna (Austria). It has no subsidiary organs but often creates Working Groups to study particular problems. One of these Working Groups studies the "communications" (complaints) received, selects those which prove the existence of persistent injustices and discrimination against women and then passes them on to the Commission. This procedure is confidential (complaints against States are not made public). Its effectiveness is quite limited, because the Commission cannot make recommendations regarding situations of violations of women's rights nor intervene before governments for humanitarian reasons.

For more information, write to:
Commission on the Status of Women,
Division for the Advancement of Women,
2, UN Plaza, DC2-12th Floor,

New York, NY 10017
Fax: (1 212) 963-3463
E-mail: daw@un.org
Internet page: http://www.un.org/womenwatch/daw/csw

3) Technical Branches: the Office of the UN High Commissioner for Human Rights (ex-Centre for Human Rights)

Since September, 1997, the secretarial work for all the UN human rights meetings and activities has been carried out by the Office of the United Nations High Commissioner for Human Rights. This post, which was created in 1993, has responsibility for putting into practice the wishes and resolutions of the United Nations with regard to human rights, for emphasizing the importance of those rights at both a national and an international level and for encouraging cooperation between States on the issue. Its work also includes representing the UN Secretary-General in meetings which deal with human rights issues and advising him on the subject, coordinating human rights programmes with the other activities of the United Nations system, and encouraging the ratification and implementation of instruments, as well as the establishment of national human rights infrastructures. The High Commissioner has a deputy, who assists him and replaces him during any periods of absence.

The Office of the High Commissioner, provides technical assistance for research work, special studies and reports, organizes meetings on human rights issues (conferences, seminars, meetings of experts), carry out field visits, prepare information and educational materials and advise governments on the subject [*see Fact Sheet No 1*]. It is based in Geneva (Switzerland), but has a small liaison office in New York (United States).

Since the end of 1997, the Office of the UN High Commissioner for Human Rights has been organized into three main branches and an Administrative Section which deals with budgetary, financial, administrative and staff management issues. The branches are the following:

Research and Right to Development, which supports the different organs which promote and protect the right to development and, on the request of the competent UN bodies, carries out the task of research, preparation of documents, reports and other materials around all issues relating to human rights. This branch also has responsibility for everything related to information, documentation, library and databases.

Support Services, which provide assistance in planning, preparation and secretarial support for all the different organs dealing with human rights (Commission, Sub-Commission, Working Groups, Committees etc.)

Activities and Programmes, which provides consultancy and technical assistance services to governments, holds responsibility for management of the different Voluntary Funds and supports the work of all the extra-conventional mechanisms of the Commission on Human Rights and ECOSOC (thematic Special Rapporteurs, offices of the High Commissioner for each continent and different offices abroad).

The Office of the UN High Commissioner for Human Rights moved in November 1998 to the Palais Wilson in Geneva. The new address is:

Palais Wilson,
52 rue des Paquis,
1201, Geneva - SWITZERLAND
Tel: (41 22) 917-9000
E-mail: webadmin.hchr@unog.ch

However the postal address for correspondence remains the same as before:

United Nations Office in Geneva
High Commissioner for Human Rights
1211, Geneva 10 -SWITZERLAND

Thus the main meetings continue to be held at the Palais des Nations.

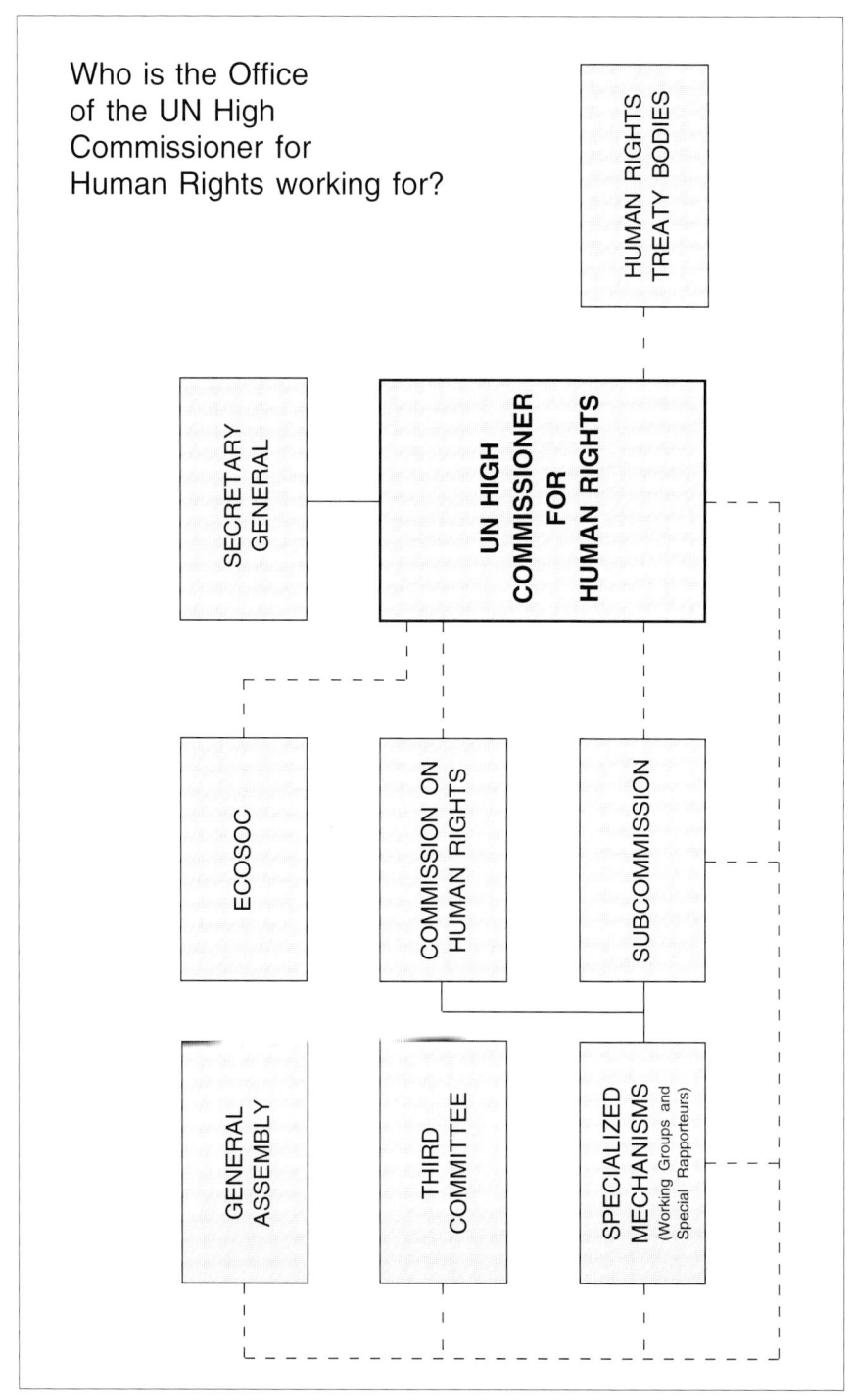

CHAPTER 2

SUBMISSION OF COMPLAINTS TO THE COMMISSION ON HUMAN RIGHTS

In Chapter 1 it was explained that the Commission on Human Rights is not an International Court of Law. It is thus not qualified to judge any particular government's conduct with regard to human rights, nor to sanction it if violations are confirmed. In spite of these limitations, a number of mechanisms have been created which enable individuals, groups and NGOs to submit complaints regarding alleged human rights violations.

The effectiveness of these different procedures varies greatly. However, over the last few years increasingly flexible, rapid and transparent practices have been established which can be very useful for the victims. None of them can replace the investigations and legal and administrative procedures which should be carried out in-country, political conditions permitting. When all is said and done, **it is at a national level that prevention of human rights violations, punishment of those responsible and compensation for victims and their families can be achieved**. Nevertheless, the mere fact that those affected have recourse to international organizations motivates governments to investigate alleged human rights violations more seriously and to enable justice to take its course, in order to maintain their image abroad.

In this chapter, we shall describe the most usual mechanisms for submitting complaints to the organs of the Commission on Human Rights. Although none of them relate specifically to indigenous peoples, indigenous organizations and individuals may obviously make use of them just like any other person or organization.

A. The 1503 Procedure

This procedure was established by ECOSOC in 1970 in order to empower the Sub-Commission and the Commission on Human Rights to receive individual complaints concerning situations which demonstrate the existence of a **consistent and widespread pattern of violation** of human rights in any particular country. These complaints are known as "communications" in the language of the United Nations. They must reflect a generalized phenomenon which affects the rights of a large number of people in a particular country over a long period of time. Complaints regarding one-off events, however serious they may be, will thus not be considered if they are the exception rather than the rule. There are other channels within the Commission, as well as a number of mechanisms established in the international Treaties, via which this type of complaint should be submitted.

The procedure is **confidential** because complaints which are accepted are dealt with in private sessions of the Sub-Commission and the Commission. Staff of the Office of the UN High Commissioner for Human Rights who are aware of the content of the complaints, along with members of the Sub-Commission and the Commission, must not divulge any information regarding either the content, the government responses or the identity of the authors, unless those involved themselves give their consent for this information to be made known.

> The aim of the procedure is to establish a dialogue between the Commission on Human Rights and the government in question. It is not a question of investigating events in depth, nor of arriving at an understanding between plaintiffs and States. Anyone initiating such a procedure by submitting a communication will thus quickly find themselves marginalized from the subsequent process. All of the actions that follow will involve only the respective organs of the United Nations which are participating at each stage, and the governments.

- *Who may make a complaint?*

Apart from direct victims and their families, **any person or group** may submit complaints within the 1503 Procedure, as long as they can demonstrate that they have direct and reliable knowledge of the events they are describing (reference to newspaper articles alone, for example, would not be sufficient). Anonymous complaints will not be considered: the author or authors must be clearly identified. The name of the person or persons making the complaint will not be made known to the relevant government, unless they agree to this being disclosed.

Complaints whose aims are inconsistent with the principles established in the Charter of the United Nations and the international instruments on human rights will not be considered (for example, communications inciting racial, ethnic, cultural or any other kind of discrimination) *[see Fact Sheet No. 7]*.

- *What information should the communication contain?*

The plaintiff must name the country which s/he considers responsible for the violations, and must describe events without resorting to language such as "bloodthirsty regime", "murderous government" or other similar expressions. Complaints may be submitted against any country, and in any of the official languages of the United Nations.

If the plaintiff is not the direct victim, as well as **identifying himself**, stating his or her relationship with the victim or victims and stating his or her information sources, s/he must give the following **information regarding the victims**: name and surname, nationality (and ethnic group or indigenous people to which they belong), date and place of birth, details of identity documents, occupation and home address. If there is any further information which may enable confirmation of the content of the complaint (newspaper articles, reports from human rights organizations, etc.), it is recommended that copies of this documentation be included. If the text of the complaint is short (two or three pages maximum), it is sufficient to send a single copy to the Office of the UN High Commissioner for Human Rights. Some organizations send weighty files with a great deal of documentation. In these cases, six complete sets of the complaint and supporting documentation should be prepared and sent.

The plaintiff **must state which rights** (civil, political, economic, social or cultural) the accused **State has violated**. In this respect, it is useful to link each violation to a particular article of the Universal Declaration of Human Rights or to the two International Covenants on Human Rights *[see Chapter 3]*. It is also important to refer **to steps already taken (successful or not)** within the country itself in order to remedy the situation. Finally, the plaintiff may explain the **purpose of his or her communication** (e.g. to get an investigation carried out; to achieve the liberation of those in detention; to obtain material compensation for the victims, etc.).

Each year, the Office of the UN High Commissioner for Human Rights receives thousand of complaints within the 1503 Procedure (more than 300,000 in 1993 alone!). Given this situation, communications should be as clear and as brief as possible. It is also useful to prepare a summary of two or three paragraphs, which sums up the most important elements, and send it along with the full complaint. This will help the staff of the Office of the UN High Commissioner for Human Rights to prepare a summary for the members of the Sub-Commission and the Commission in good time. Finally, as the procedure is very slow, it is recommended to send yearly updates on the situation.

> All complaints sent to any of the organs of the United Nations system are passed on to the Office of the UN High Commissioner for Human Rights, who will process them according to the rules of the 1503 Procedure. In order to save time, it is advisable to send them directly, and if possible before May each year, to:
> Office of the United Nations High Commissioner for Human Rights,
> United Nations office at Genève
> 1211, Genève 10 - Switzerland
> Fax: (4122) 917 9011

Communications received by the Office of the UN High Commissioner for Human Rights after May will not be considered by the Sub-Commission until the following year.

- *How will complaints submitted under this Procedure be processed within the United Nations?*

The 1503 Procedure theoretically comprises six stages, making it a long and complex mechanism. Very few cases reach the fifth stage (the Commission on Human Rights) and virtually none make use of the sixth stage (ECOSOC).

The steps are the following:

1) The Office of the UN High Commissioner for Human Rights makes an initial assessment of the complaints. If the information is incomplete, or offensive language is used, it writes to the plaintiffs requesting further information or asking that the communication be rewritten. If the information is complete, serious and credible, the Office acknowledges receipt and informs the plaintiff that the complaint will be passed on to the Sub-Commission, the Commission and the respective governments. **There is then no further communication between the United Nations and the plaintiffs**. No information is given regarding the stage which the communication has reached, nor regarding the reply of the government concerning the allegations made.

The Office of the UN High Commissioner for Human Rights then prepares summaries of the complaints and each month draws up a confidential country by country list, which is sent to all members of the Sub-Commission and the Commission. A copy of the original complaint is also sent to the relevant government, with the name of the plaintiff removed. Thus, if a relative who does not wish to be identified by the government sends a communication under the 1503 Procedure, s/he should avoid repeating the family tie that links him or her with the direct victim (expressions such as "my father", "my husband" or "my daughter" should be avoided because it is very difficult to remove these if they are mentioned many times in the document).

The government has a period of three or four months in which to reply to the allegations. No government is obliged to respond but most do so because their silence would draw the attention of the Commission, which could then decide to examine the human rights situation in that country more closely. If after four months the Office has not received a reply from the government, another note is sent with a summary of the case and any further information that may have been received in the meantime.

2) At the end of July each year, **the Sub-Commission's Working Group on Communications** studies the cases on the monthly lists that have been drawn up between May of the previous year and April of the current year and considers the governments' responses. This Working Group meets in closed session (not open to the public) for two weeks. It selects a small number of communications which seem to demonstrate the existence of a systematic and widespread violations of human rights in certain countries and refers them to the Sub-Commission, which deals with them under Item 9 of its Agenda ('Communications concerning human rights…').

3) In August, **the Sub-Commission** studies the complaints in plenary (but closed) session and decides which „situations" are particularly worthy of being referred to the Commission on Human Rights. At this level, individual complaints are no longer considered, but rather a package of complaints which reveal an overall pattern of human rights violations in a particular country (thus reference is no longer made to "communications" but to "situations"). About ten situations are generally referred to the Commission each year. Some cases will be retained for study in the next session, others will be rejected, and others sent back to the Working Group on Communications for further analysis. At this stage, the Sub-Commission may consider other relevant information which does not appear in the communication. When the Sub-Commission decides to send a situation to the Commission, it informs the respective government and requests that they present their observations in writing to the Commission.

4) The communications and comments of the governments are then studied by the **Commission's Working Group on Situations**. This WG

meets annually for one week, in closed session, prior to the Commission's annual session. It only recommends a small number of situations, and sends the text of the suggested recommendations to the relevant governments in advance.

5) The **Commission** requests the attendance of government representatives at a private session in which the case will be discussed, in order to reply to the allegations made and to answer questions.

In practice, the Commission has developed its own methods for applying the 1503 Procedure. It generally decides on one of the following options: a) to drop an issue when there is no longer any reason to continue examining it; b) to continue to examine the situation year on year, receiving new information from the government and the plaintiffs; c) to appoint an independent expert to establish direct contact with the government and people of the country, collect information from different sources, negotiate with government representatives and propose ways of eliminating human rights violations, or d) to suspend confidential examination of the issue in order to deal with it within the framework of Public Procedure 1235.

> The only information which is made public during this process are the names of the countries which are being studied by the Commission under the 1503 Procedure and those where a confidential examination of the human rights situation has been suspended. These names appear in the Commission's annual report, under Point 12 (XII).

It is clear that the 1503 Procedure is a long one, with many drawbacks, particularly with regard to urgent cases. Nevertheless, **it can be used to denounce the human rights situation in countries which have not ratified the existing international instruments**. Before sending a complaint under the 1503 Procedure it is worth considering each individual case carefully to see whether there are more speedy and effective alternatives available, either at an international or a regional level.

B. Public Procedure 1235

In 1967, ECOSOC approved Resolution 1235, authorising the Commission on Human Rights and the Sub-Commission to study information regarding clear violations of human rights and fundamental freedoms

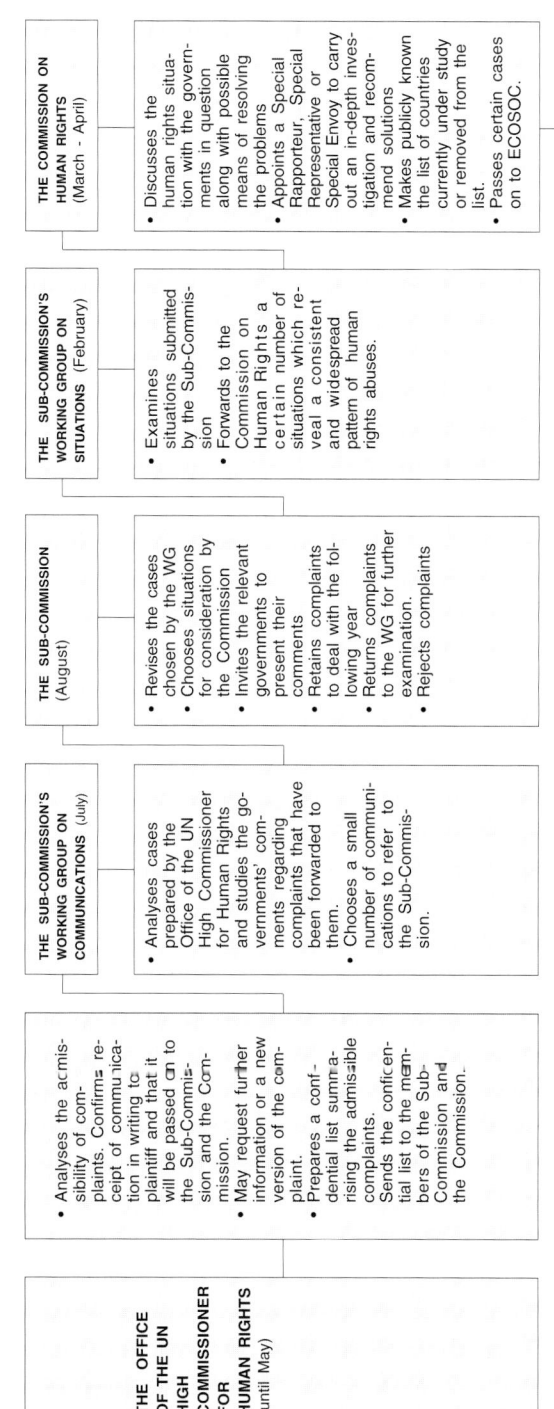

(including racial discrimination). This issue has now become Item 6 of the Sub-Commission's agenda, and Item 12 of the agenda of the Commission on Human Rights. In both fora, the issue is discussed in open session and NGOs in consultative status with ECOSOC may present written information in advance and participate orally with regard to the relevant agenda point *[see 'Some practical issues relating to NGO participation... ', in Chapter 1].*

After studying the information received, the Commission may authorise an in-depth study of those situations "which reveal a consistent pattern of violations of human rights" and subsequently presents a report and recommendations to ECOSOC. It may also approve a resolution condemning the situation and proposing ways in which to resolve it.

> The advantage of the public procedure over the 1503 Procedure is that complaints are discussed before members of every organ, observers and a large public. The press is immediately informed and circulates the information received. This constitutes a strong form of political pressure on the government in question. It furthermore serves as a way of informing world opinion and gaining sympathy for the cause of the victims of human rights violations.

C. Specialized extra-conventional mechanisms (Special Rapporteurs, Experts and Working Groups)

Since 1978, the Commission on Human Rights has created mechanisms for receiving all kinds of information regarding phenomena which constitute violations of fundamental rights and freedoms. Some of these mechanisms investigate specific practices such as torture, enforced disappearances and arbitrary detention throughout the world (these are the so-called **'thematic' mechanisms or mandates**). Others study the situation in particular countries where massive violations of human rights exist (the so-called **'country' mechanisms or mandates**).

> *The main powers of the Commission's specialized mechanisms:*
> - to receive general information (including complaints and newspaper sources) regarding serious human rights violations. This information may be provided by governments, specialized agencies of the UN system, NGOs, individuals (victims, families, friends or simple witnesses) .

> - to study the existence and scope of these practices in order to determine why they occur, how they could be prevented and to remedy their consequences.
> - to put the victims or their families in contact with the relevant government so that the alleged situations may be investigated and efforts made to resolve them.
> - to intercede before governments with regard to urgent cases, for humanitarian reasons, in order to protect the life and physical and mental integrity of alleged victims.
> - to make general recommendations to the Commission and governments regarding the measures which should be adopted in order to eliminate these practices.

The specialized mechanisms are the responsibility of Working Groups composed of five members, or of Experts, Special Representatives or Special Rapporteurs. The people appointed by the Commission are independent experts in the field of human rights. They will receive all types of statements as long as they are not anonymous complaints or information which is impossible to corroborate from other sources. They then request clarification from the respective governments, regardless of whether they have ratified the relevant international Treaties or not (this is why they are known as "**extra-conventional mechanisms**"). Although these mechanisms were originally established for a limited period of time only, in practice they have become permanent.

The function of the Commission's thematic mechanisms is not to determine whether a human rights violation has been committed or not, nor to find out who is responsible, but to act as investigators, collecting as much information as possible and endeavouring to establish channels of communication between governments and the citizens whose rights are being violated. Methods have gradually developed which enable them to act rapidly and effectively: **receipt of complaints** and their transmission to the government in question for a response; **urgent messages** to governments in cases where the lives and physical and mental integrity of one or a number of people are in danger, and **field-missions** to see for themselves the situation of the country. These visits are undertaken by invitation only or with the express approval of the authorities.

> *What is the minimum information that a complaint should include?*
> - full identity of the plaintiff (name and surname, identity card, date and place of birth, nationality, occupation, address, telephone and fax number, if applicable).
> - full identity of the victim (if different from the plaintiff). Indicate, where appropriate, to which indigenous peoples s/he belongs, and, when appropiate, if she is a pregnant woman.
> - the circumstances of the alleged event: place, exact date (or, in the case of people detained or disappeared without witness, date and place where they were last seen), and a complete description of events, mentioning all previous circumstances which could be linked to the event (threats, persecution, victim's activities - political, union, professional or other - which could be related to the event), identification of the alleged perpetrators and possible witnesses.
> - methods undertaken to seek redress at national level: complaints made to the police or any other competent authority, recourse to protection or habeas corpus, etc.
> - any additional information: newspaper articles; reports from human rights NGOs which have taken up the case; statements by people linked to the government who admit responsibility for such actions or who justify them; a copy of the relevant national legislation which the government invokes to justify its actions, etc.

The extra-conventional mechanisms will receive complaints even if recourse to internal mechanisms may not have been exhausted, or if the same issue is being dealt with by another regional or international body. In accordance with Resolution 1993/30 of the Commission on Human Rights **all thematic mechanisms must pay special attention to the situation of indigenous peoples**.

The Commission's specialized 'country' mechanisms:

These are experts, chosen in their personal capacity, which the Commission appoints to supervise the human rights situation in countries where serious violations are known to occur. The first was the Working Group set up in 1974 with regard to Chile. Another was established in 1975 to monitor the situation in South Africa.

The Commission authorises them to receive all kinds of information and to make in-country visits in order to dialogue with the authorities and with non-governmental organizations. As these visits are not always authorised by the government, they often meet elsewhere with individuals and groups wishing to give statements, either in Geneva or New York, or in countries neighbouring the one under examination. Much weight is given to information provided by eyewitnesses or from impartial and reliable sources and confidentiality is maintained when witnesses request it. They also receive written information presented by the specialized agencies of the UN system and by NGOs.

They furthermore endeavour to find out the opinion of the government through its direct replies or through studying statements and documents published by official sources or pro-government communication channels. Before presenting their reports to the Commission, they usually request the opinion of the government under scrutiny with regard to the interpretations, conclusions and recommendations included within their reports.

The thematic mechanisms of the Commission and the Sub-Commission:

1) The Working Group on Enforced or Involuntary Disappearances

- *What it does, where and when it sits in session:*

This WG was set up by the Commission in 1980, with an annual mandate. Since 1992, this has been renewed at three-yearly intervals. It meets three times per year in private, for between five to eight days each time. Two of its annual meetings are held in Geneva whilst the third is held in New York. Government representatives, NGOs, families and witnesses are usually invited to participate in these meetings. With the authorisation of the respective governments, they also undertake missions to different countries.

- *How it works:*

The main function of the WG is to establish a means of communication between the families of the disappeared and the government, with the aim of locating disappeared people or finding out what has happened to them and, as far as possible, of saving the lives of those recently disappeared. It also deals with the issue of the children of disappeared parents. It undertakes an enormous amount of work: in its first seven years of existence (1980-1987) it transmitted around 15,000 cases of disappearances to some forty governments. Only a very few of the cases are ever conclusively resolved. Its effectiveness is greater when dealing with cases of recent disappearances.

The WG receives information regarding disappearances, requests the cooperation of the government in the investigation of the whereabouts of disappeared people and, in recent cases (those less than three months old), sends urgent messages to governments requesting they look into the matter and establish the whereabouts of these people. Urgent interventions are made by telegram, telephone or fax immediately on receipt of the complaint.

- *Submission of complaints to the WG on Disappearances:*

The WG only deals with people who appear to have been detained by government officials or organised groups or individuals acting on behalf of the government or with its knowledge. It does not deal with complaints regarding disappearances attributed to terrorist or insurgency movements, nor does it investigate those which occur during periods of international armed conflict, as these are the responsibility of the International Committee of the Red Cross. Nor does it deal with cases in which the disappeared person is known to have been assassinated. Such information is passed on to the Special Rapporteur on Extra-Judicial, Summary or Arbitrary Executions.

Complaints can be made by family or friends of the victims or by non-governmental and humanitarian organizations acting on behalf of the interested party and which are in close contact with the direct family. They must be written, or may be a tape recording accompanied by a written summary of its content. The Office of the UN High Commissioner for Human Rights provides a form for the submission of complaints [*doc. CHR/WGEID/1987*].

- *What does the WG do with the complaints it receives?*

If the complaint contains the minimum information necessary, the Working Group passes it on to the government so that they may investigate it and provide information regarding the results of their search. When the plaintiff requests that his or her identity should not be revealed, personal information is not mentioned. In order to protect the safety of plaintiffs, the WG may even demand „rapid intervention" on the part of the government in the event of intimidation or reprisals against them.

The government's response is then studied by the WG and communicated to the plaintiff so that s/he may comment or make any necessary clarifications. Any new information which the plaintiff has regarding the whereabouts of the disappeared person must be immediately passed on to the WG in order to facilitate follow-up to the complaint and to avoid unnecessary efforts being deployed.

The WG considers that a case has been clarified when the government (or the plaintiff or another non-governmental source) indicates where the disappeared person is (dead or alive), provided that the plaintiff accepts this information or does not contradict it within a period of six months. The governments in question are reminded once every year by the WG of cases that have not yet been clarified.

> On the recommendation of the Working Group on Involuntary or Enforced Disappearances, the **Declaration on the Protection of All Persons from Enforced Disappearance** was drawn up and adopted by the GA in 1992. National legislation should now incorporate these standards and consider that all actions aimed at carrying out or tolerating a disappearance constitute a grave offence which must be judged and punished under criminal and civil law. The Working Group on the question of the Administration of Justice has also drawn up a **draft Convention on Enforced Disappearances** which is being studied by the Commission.

For more information, see Fact Sheet No. 6 (Rev. 2) or the UN's human rights Internet web site or contact the Office of the UN High Commissioner for Human Rights on telephone number: (41 22) 917-9289 or fax number: 917-9006.

2) The Special Rapporteur for Extrajudicial, Summary or Arbitrary Executions

- *What s/he does, where and when to contact him/her:*

The mandate of this Special Rapporteur was established by the Commission in 1982, and is renewed every three years. Its aim is to study cases of summary or arbitrary execution, to respond effectively to information indicating that arbitrary executions in a particular country are possible or imminent and to provide the Commission with information regarding the existence and extent of this practice. In order to carry out his/her work, the Special Rapporteur travels to Geneva three times per year, at various times.

- *How s/he works:*

For the Special Rapporteur, an execution is summary or arbitrary when the victim has not been judged or condemned by a competent court or when the minimum guarantees established by international law have not been respected during a trial or when the person's rights have been violated. Within the mandate are thus included murders carried out by order of a government or with its complicity or tolerance, the death of a person in custody as a result of torture, mistreatment or an excessive use of force, the implementation of the death penalty on minors, expectant women, young mothers or the mentally retarded, the actions of the „death squads" or groups not under the control of the government, the expulsion of people to countries where their lives are in danger, genocide and, in times of armed conflict, civilian deaths caused by members of the armed or security forces. Since 1993, special attention has been given to the issue of child executions and to the violation of the right to life as a consequence of the violent repression of people participating in demonstrations and other peaceful public meetings.

The Special Rapporteur **requests and receives information** from governments and NGOs in consultative status with ECOSOC only. The NGOs with which s/he collaborates most closely are Amnesty International, the World Council of Churches, Pax Romana, the International Commission of Jurists, the International Federation of Human Rights and the International Association of Democratic Lawyers. S/he also meets with interested parties and other UN organs to analyse concrete situations and makes visits to different countries on the invitation of governments in order to collect information.

- *Submission of complaints to the SR for Summary Executions:*

Complaints may refer to individual and isolated incidents, to situations affecting a certain number of people (such as the massacre of the inhabitants of a community) or to situations of generalised executions. In order to be able to act effectively, the Special Rapporteur requires information to be sent which contains the minimum information previously mentioned.

- *What does the SR do with the complaints received?*
- If an execution has already been carried out, s/he communicates the complaints to the government, requesting that it provides information regarding the official investigation that was implemented and the action the courts took in punishing those responsible. The Rapporteur may then request further clarification of the replies received, but s/he does not demand that the government presents evidence of its actions, nor does s/he ask the plaintiff to comment or to make observations on the government's replies.
- If an execution is imminent, s/he sends urgent messages to the government requesting that international standards and the rights of the condemned be respected, or requesting further information on the case. On occasions, the Special Rapporteur may request postponement of the sentence, or clemency on the part of the authorities. **All complaints requiring urgent action on the part of the Special Rapporteur must be presented via an NGO with consultative status** recognised by ECOSOC and must contain information indicating the arbitrary nature

of the execution (violation of the procedural rights of the condemned or of his/her fundamental rights).

When information received from non-governmental sources and the replies obtained from the government are clearly in contradiction with each other, the Special Rapporteur may also request that the government invites him/her to visit the country and to check in situ what the prevailing circumstances are. If the Special Rapporteur considers that the case has not been resolved, s/he sends follow-up letters to the government requesting up-to-date information on the investigations being undertaken.

The Special Rapporteur can be contacted by writing to the Office of the UN High Commissioner for Human Rights or calling (41 22) 917-3353/917-3875. Fax number: (41 22) 917-9006.

3) The Special Rapporteur on Torture

- *What s/he does:*

Since 1985, the Special Rapporteur has actively searched for and received information provided by governments, intergovernmental organizations, NGOs and individuals with regard to issues relating to torture. Established with an initial one year mandate, it is now renewed every three years.

- *How s/he works:*

The Special Rapporteur considers torture as "any act by which severe pain or suffering, whether physical or mental, is intentionally inflicted on a person", provided that this suffering is not related to a legal punishment or sentence, "for the purpose of obtaining from that person, or a third person, information or a confession", in order to "punish the person for an act they have, or are suspected of having committed", in order to intimidate them "or for any reason based on any type of discrimination". These actions constitute cases of torture only when committed by government officials, people exercising public function or in the service of government officials (for example, paramilitary or security forces). According to the Special Rapporteur, the prohibition of torture is **an obligation on the part of all States**, even those who have not ratified any of the relevant Treaties on the subject. Punishment of those guilty of acts of torture is thus a fundamental means of prevention and is the responsibility of the executive and judicial authorities of all countries.

> One of its main functions is to advise governments on ways in which to prevent torture. Its aim is not to condemn any particular State but to draw the attention of its authorities to the subject, requesting them to consider the issue and, if the complaints are proven, to guarantee that those guilty will be punished and the victims compensated.

The Special Rapporteur **maintains contact with the interested parties** several times per year, in Geneva. There are no fixed dates and so to request a meeting contact should firstly be made with his/her secretary, telephone number: (41 22) 917-9205 or fax number (41 22) 917-9006.

On the invitation of the respective governments, the Special Rapporteur visits different countries in order to carry out **field missions** during which s/he meets government representatives and NGOs and visits detention centres, subsequently presenting reports on the measures being undertaken by the respective governments to eliminate torture. S/he also **makes urgent calls** to governments in cases where a person in detention is being tortured or runs the imminent risk of being tortured.

- *The submission of complaints to the Special Rapporteur:*

The Rapporteur on Torture will accept complaints from NGOs, whether they have consultative status with ECOSOC or not, provided they are considered credible. This means that they will check that the necessary information about the victim is included and that this information is consistent and complete, in order to facilitate the investigation and ensure its effectiveness.

Subjective factors are also considered: the quality of the sources - whether it is the victim him or herself, a member of the family or a close acquaintance -, although very often complaints are submitted by NGOs. In this case, it is a question of ascertaining whether the NGO is well known, if it works in a responsible manner and if its information is reliable. Information is considered credible when it is received from two different sources.

- *What does the SR do with complaints that are accepted?*

Recognised complaints are passed on to the State in question, requesting that they commence an investigation into events and that they provide information regarding the means they have adopted to avoid torture or to punish those responsible. The SR has established a precedent by which the identity of its informants will not be revealed, in order to avoid exposing them to the risk of reprisals. S/he also initiates urgent actions with governments on behalf of people who risk reprisals for having cooperated with the human rights organs of the United Nations.

If the situation is not an urgent one, the Rapporteur collects together all the cases which have occurred in any particular country and, once or twice a year, sends this information to the government in question. Copies of the governments' replies are later forwarded to the plaintiffs with requests for their comments. If new and relevant information is subsequently received from the plaintiffs, the Special Rapporteur may forward the case to the government a second time.

In **cases of urgent** appeal, the Special Rapporteur gets in touch with the government within 24 hours of receiving the complaint, either by telephone, telegram or fax requesting a guarantee regarding the physical and mental integrity of the alleged victim. S/he may also intervene in cases where a person is about to be extradited or repatriated to a country where s/he may face torture.

> Since 1981, the United Nations has a **Voluntary Fund for Victims of Torture** [see Fact Sheet No. 4], which provides financial, legal and humanitarian aid to the victims of torture and their families, anywhere in the world. This Voluntary Fund provides assistance for a number of different programmes (for example, international centres for the rehabilitation of torture victims, programmes of medical and psychological treatment, study grants, professional training workshops etc). For more information write to:
>
> The Voluntary Fund for Victims of Torture,
> Office of the UN High Commissioner for Human Rights,
> 1211, Geneva 10,
> Switzerland.
> Or call the following numbers:
> (41 22) 917-9266; Fax: (41 22) 917-9017.

4) The Working Group on the Arbitrary Deprivation of Freedom

- *What it does, where and when it functions:*

In 1991, the Commission set up a Working Group on arbitrary detention to investigate complaints regarding detentions imposed in an arbitrary fashion or which were incompatible with current international law. For the Working Group, a detention is considered arbitrary, for example, when a person is taken into custody by the authorities for exercising any of the rights which are guaranteed by the Universal Declaration of Human Rights and the International Covenants, such as the right to a fair trial, to non-discrimination, and to the fundamental freedoms of movement, of requesting asylum in another country, of opinion and expression, of thought, conscience and religion, of peaceful assembly and association, and of participating in the political life of his or her country. The Working Group also studies cases of people in administrative custody (with no charge or trial pending) or who continue to be detained despite an amnesty or despite their sentence having been served. However, it does not deal with situations of international armed conflict.

In 1997, the Commission decided to change the Working Group's name to the Working Group on the Arbitrary Deprivation of Freedom. Thus any situation in which a detention exists as a result of a judicial sentence falls outside the mandate of this Working Group, as long as the sentence was imposed in accordance with national and international standards regarding the due process.

It meets three times a year in Geneva, in sessions that last between five and eight working days, and it works in close cooperation with the other thematic or country mechanisms, occasionally accompanying them on joint missions.

- *How it works:*

Its mandate authorises it to **investigate complaints** received from governments, intergovernmental organizations, NGOs and individuals (this means that, as opposed to the previously mentioned mechanisms, **it can decide whether complaints are justified or not and whether governments are responsible** for arbitrary detentions). It can also initiate its own investigations. It receives written information from either the victims or their families or representatives.

The WG **initiates urgent actions** with governments when the life or health of a detained person is in danger because of that detention. It then requests that the authorities consider the possibility of freeing the detained person or providing them with the necessary medical treatment, on humanitarian grounds. The Working Group makes regular in-country visits, on the invitation of the respective governments.

- *Submission of complaints to the WG on the Arbitrary Deprivation of Freedom:*

When sending a complaint to the WG, the minimum information previously mentioned must be provided, along with the reasons given by the authorities to justify the detention, and the national legislation that applies to the case. The plaintiff must also indicate the reasons why s/he considers the detention to be arbitrary. An example of a complaint can be found on the Internet. For urgent actions, send a fax to the secretary or an e-mail to the following address: mschmidt.hchr@unog.ch.

- *What does the WG do with the complaints received?*

Once a complaint is accepted by the Working Group, the case is presented to the relevant government, requesting them to investigate and respond within 90 days. On receiving the government's response, the WG forwards it to the plaintiffs requesting their comments, or any further information they may have regarding the case. Finally, the WG informs the government of its opinions and recommendations and publishes these opinions in an annex to the Commission's annual report. If it considers that the detention is not an arbitrary one, if there is insufficient information for the case to be held pending or if the person is freed, the WG may close the file on the case, although it reserves the right to decide whether the deprivation of freedom was arbitrary or not. The WG also adopts deliberations on questions of a more general nature, with the aim of setting criteria to define the circumstances under which the deprivation of freedom may be considered arbitrary.

> If the Working Group considers a case of arbitrary deprivation of freedom to be proven, it makes recommendations to the government to remedy the situation and to bring it into line with the standards established under international law. These recommendations appear in the Commission's annual report. This mechanism is original because, by including the possibility of investigating and deciding whether the detention is arbitrary or not itself, the WG acts virtually as a court, although it is not able to impose sentences.

To provide information to the Working Group on the Arbitrary Deprivation of Freedom, write to the Office of the UN High Commissioner for Human Rights, or call (41 22) 917-9258 or send a fax to 917-9006.

5) The Special Rapporteur on the sale of children, child prostitution and child pornography

This Special Rapporteur was appointed in 1990, on the suggestion of the Sub-Commission's Working Group on Contemporary Forms of Slavery. Its mandate was initially an annual one, but since 1992 it has been renewed every three years.

- *What it does and how it works:*

The Special Rapporteur must **examine reliable information** from governments, specialized agencies of the UN, intergovernmental organizations, NGOs (with or without ECOSOC consultative status) and even from newspaper sources regarding the problem of the sale of children for commercial gain or for their use in prostitution or pornography. It thus works in close cooperation with the Committee on the Rights of the Child *[see Chapter 3]*, with the Sub-Commission's Working Group on Contemporary Forms of Slavery *[see Chapter 1]*, and with other agencies of the UN system (UNICEF, WHO, ILO and INTERPOL).

The Special Rapporteur may also **visit countries** on the invitation of the respective governments. A system of direct contact with governments and NGOs has been established for the processing of routine complaints and for rapid action in urgent cases.

- *The submission of complaints to the Special Rapporteur*

When the information available is precise and reliable, the Special Rapporteur tries to clarify the situation by sending the complaints directly to the relevant governments (for example, in cases of involuntary child brides or networks of child traffickers). The replies are then sent to the plaintiffs who have the opportunity of commenting on them and providing further information which may help to resolve the case.

Complaints can be sent by families or NGOs to the Office of the UN High Commissioner for Human Rights, by post or fax: (41 22) 917-9006

6) Other specialized mechanisms of the Commission

The Commission has a number of other Working Groups or thematic Special Rapporteurs which deal with issues of interest to indigenous peoples. It would take too long to describe them all here, but more detailed information can be requested from the Office of the UN High Commissioner for Human Rights. Alternatively, the UN's human rights web site on the Internet can be consulted at http://www.unhcr.ch.

Some of these mechanisms are very new, and their working methods are thus still being studied and improved, drawing on the accumulated experience of other older procedures. In general, the new mandates are authorised to receive - and even to actively search for - information from a variety of sources; they are authorised to receive complaints and follow these up and there is provision for field visits and urgent calls to governments.

There follows a partial list of these mechanisms:

- **the Special Rapporteur on Religious Intolerance.** Since 1986 this SR has been examining the extent to which the Declaration on the elimination of all forms of intolerance and of discrimination based on religion or belief is being adhered to.

- **the Special Rapporteur on the Promotion and Protection of the Right to Freedom of Opinion and Expression.** This SR, appointed in 1993, collects together information on cases of discrimination, threats or acts of violence against people trying to exercise or promote the right to freedom of opinion and expression (for example, journalists threatened for voicing an opinion or for providing the public with information).

- **the Special Rapporteur on Violence against Women.** Appointed in 1994, this SR collects together information regarding the different practices which constitute acts of violence against women (women in situations of armed conflict, violence based on sexual discrimination, systematic rape and involuntary pregnancy, sexual slavery, etc.).

- **the Special Rapporteur on Mercenaries:** this SR has been studying the problem of the use of mercenaries as a means of impeding the exercise of the right of peoples to self-determination since 1987.

- **the Special Rapporteur on Contemporary Forms of Racism, Racial Discrimination, Xenophobia** (hatred of foreigners) **and Related Intolerance.** Appointed in 1993, this SR has responsibility for studying a large number of situations, including both the recent expressions of racism and violence against foreigners and migrant workers in the developed world as well as the situation of indigenous peoples and ethnic, cultural, linguistic and religious minorities suffering from different forms of discrimination and racism.

CHAPTER 3

SUBMITTING COMPLAINTS TO THE CONVENTIONAL BODIES OF THE UN

A. Introduction

A **'conventional mechanism'** is a supervisory organ established by an international Treaty, that is, by a legal standard adopted freely by States. In most cases, the Treaty itself creates a special body to monitor fulfilment of its measures. Often, this "treaty body" is authorised to receive complaints regarding violations of the rights protected by the Treaty in question within the States which have ratified it.

In the introduction to this chapter, we will first of all define what is meant by an international instrument, what the treaty bodies are, how they work and how NGOs can make use of the UN's conventional mechanisms. There follow six international instruments and their respective treaty bodies, with information on how access can be gained to each one. Finally, we will look at another four international instruments which deal with rights of relevance to indigenous peoples: the right to protection against genocide, the right to self-determination, the right to development and the right to peace.

We also take the opportunity to introduce some information on the recently approved International Criminal Court.

1) The international instruments

The Charter of the United Nations commits member States to the promotion and protection of human rights. With this in mind, by 1947 the UN had already begun to draw up the texts of future international standards. In general, there are three stages in the creation of new international legislation:
- First, the need for standards must be demonstrated by gathering information on situations of abuse and denial of the rights of people or communities. This information is drawn from complaints and reports submitted by victims, NGOs or governments, or from studies undertaken by Working Groups, Special Rapporteurs or experts of the Commission on Human Rights and its Sub-Commission *[see Chapter 2]*.
- Secondly, texts are prepared which outline the general principles which should guide government actions towards its citizens. Once the States have reached adequate consensus on the content of the general principles to be proclaimed, a **Declaration** is adopted.
- Finally, although this stage is not always reached, more concrete and binding legal texts are drawn up for the States adopting them

(known as 'States Parties'). This kind of legal text, which the States Parties commit themselves to formally fulfilling, is known as a Treaty. There are a number of different types: a **Bill** a **Charter or a Covenant** (terms used for important instruments of a general nature), a **Convention** (relating to one or more human rights), or a **Protocol** (which revises the terms of Bills, Covenants and Conventions, or adds further measures to them). All of these documents describe in detail the rights which they protect, the limitations or restrictions to their application and the responsibilities taken on by the States Parties.

Together, the Declarations and Treaties drawn up to proclaim and guarantee rights are known as **international instruments**.

The difference between a Declaration and a Treaty

A Declaration is an expression of ideals, of applicable universal moral rules which it would be desirable to achieve but which are not, in principle, binding. On the other hand, Treaties clearly set out within their text what obligations the States which are ratifying them are committing themselves to (that is, the **guarantees** which will ensure protection of the rights proclaimed). Thus the moral commitment which is assumed on adopting a Declaration is strengthened and consolidated with the drawing up of a Treaty.

The guarantees result in the **mechanisms for implementation** of the Treaty: internally, the States Parties commit themselves to respecting its terms, amending national legislation where necessary and providing its citizens with a system through which they can appeal to the legal and administrative authorities; internationally, they are obliged to report periodically to the treaty body on progress achieved and difficulties encountered in the application of these standards. **Treaties thus become standards of a nature that is above national legislation** for the countries which have ratified them.

Ratification of an international Treaty

In order to become a new instrument of international law, all Treaties and Declarations drawn up by the UN must before anything else be adopted through Resolutions or Recommendations of the corresponding legislative body (General Assembly, Conference of States, etc.). In the case of Treaties, the **signing** by representatives of the States which have decided to take part in this new instrument then takes place and, subsequently, the **ratification** according to the procedures of each country. For a Covenant, Protocol or Convention to enter into force in a country and be enforceable on a government, it is not enough that it has been **signed**; it must also have been **ratified** by its authorities.

Any State which did not **sign** the Treaty at the time of its adoption may subsequently **access** to it, which has the same effect as **ratification**. When a Treaty is signed, ratified or accessed to, the States have the right to submit **reservations and/or interpretative declarations** on some Articles, thus limiting the obligations they are undertaking, as long as such reservations and declarations are not incompatible with the objective of the instrument itself.

The United Nations periodically publishes lists of the States which have ratified the international human rights instruments, including the reservations and observations made by each State Party. *[The Department of Public Information publishes these lists as document NU.ST/LEG/SER/E/10 (always ask for the most up-to-date version). It is also possible to check ratification status at the Internet site of the UN High Commissioner for Human Rights: www.unhchr.ch.].*

INTERNATIONAL HUMAN RIGHTS TREATIES	
Of a general nature:BILL, CHARTER or COVENANT	Relating to a specific number of rights: COVENTION, OPTIONAL PROTOCOL
<ul><li>They define the rights which they protect and the limitations on their application;</li><li>They establish guarantees for fulfilment on the part of the States.</li></ul>	

2) The Treaty-monitoring bodies

In order to supervise the States' fulfilment of the obligations they have assumed by ratifying international human rights Treaties, special bodies normally known as Committees are established. It should be noted that not all of the Treaties provide for the creation of a Committee to supervise their fulfilment (such is the case, for example, with the Convention on the Prevention and Punishment of the Crime of Genocide), nor do all of the Committees within the international system of protection of human rights derive their existence from a Treaty (the Special Committee on Decolonization, for example, was set up to monitor the application of the Declaration on the Granting of Independence to Colonial Countries and Peoples).

These Committees are made up of human rights experts who act in their personal capacity (at least, in principle, although not always in reality). When deciding on their composition, the UN tries to achieve a geographical balance and representation from different legal systems and forms of civilisation.

The main role of the Committees is the supervision of the application of the measures of implementation anticipated for each Treaty. Two complementary mechanisms exist for this: an **examination of the periodic reports** provided by the States Parties and, in some cases only, the receipt and follow up of **complaints or communications** regarding lack of fulfilment of the contractual obligations of a State Party.

The Committees can also formulate **suggestions and recommendations** of a general nature which apply to no State in particular but to the different Articles of the Treaty, enabling their interpretation to be refined. The precise content of the protected rights and the States' obligations are thus clarified. The Committees' suggestions and recommendations may also refer to their own working methods, to the requirements for the submission of regular reports or to special issues which they decide to discuss.

The submission of periodic reports
The States Parties to an international Treaty must submit periodic reports on the way in which they are putting the measures of the Treaty into practice. These reports are **compulsory, public** and made known a certain time in advance. The Treaty bodies study this information, supplementing it and comparing it, in general, with other sources. As each report is dealt with, government representatives may be questioned by members of the Committee in order to clarify any points or to provide further information. Occasionally, they may be asked to submit a new report, even before the date established for this. The Committee then draws its conclusions on the reports it has studied, which may include recommendations on how application of the Treaty on the part of States Parties could be improved. When any country is found to be in violation of the rights protected by the Treaty, the Committee may show its concern or its desire that the situation be corrected through requesting the adoption of a number of measures.

The Office of the UN Centre for Human Rights and the United Nations Institute for Training and Research (UNITAR) have published a Manual on Human Rights Reporting aimed at national public officials in charge of writing these reports. The Manual analyses general aspects of report presentation and the requirements demanded by six international human rights instruments. In each case, the contribution NGOs can make into the process is noted. The Manual is an important tool for human rights NGOs. It is published as document HR/PUB/91/1.

3) The submission of individual complaints

Some Treaties provide for the possibility of submitting complaints to the corresponding treaty body regarding failure to comply with its terms. In theory, these communications may be submitted by another State Party or by individuals. However, to date, within the framework of the United Nations system, a case has never arisen of one State denouncing another for failure to fulfil the terms of a Treaty.

The mechanisms enabling individuals to submit complaints against States can be found in the text of the Treaty itself, or in a separate document. In the first case, it is normally a prior condition that the State Party "recognises the **authority of the Committee**" to receive complaints from individuals (that is, that they accept that their conduct may be evaluated by the Committee). In the second case, this possibility is included in an Optional Protocol which the States Parties may, if they so desire, ratify in addition to the Treaty to which it relates.

It is important to be aware that the submission of an individual communication to a Committee does not give rise to immediate action on their part. Firstly, the Committee has to decide whether the complaint is admissible or not. The requirements for admissibility are generally specified in the text of the instrument itself *[see Fact Sheet No. 7, which includes a model communication]*.

> In general terms, the requirements for admissibility for a communication are the following:
> a) that it is not anonymous and that the victim or victims may be identified;
> b) that the complaint is made by the victim, or by a close family member or a third person who can justify their links with the victim, with reasons as to why the victim cannot submit the case him or herself;
> c) that the plaintiff has exhausted internal legal channels or can demonstrate that he or she did not have access to them or that they are too slow;
> d) that the plaintiff is not processing the same case through another intergovernmental, regional or international legal body;
> e) that the complaint is well-founded and accompanied by all documentation possible;
> f) that it is not written in a language which would be offensive to the State whose conduct is in question.

If the Committee decides that the complaint is admissible, it forwards it to the State in question, requesting it to respond to the charges formulated and asking it to provide all necessary information to resolve the issue. The Government's response and the Committee's decision are forwarded to the plaintiff, who then has the possibility of contesting it and sending more information in support of his or her complaint. If the State establishes that the rights of the plaintiff have been violated, it must inform the Committee what measures it has adopted to correct and remedy the situation.

The Committee then presents its **observations** and **decisions** to the State Party and the plaintiff with regard to whether there has been a violation of a particular article of the Treaty or not and includes a summary of the action undertaken in its annual report. This is an important way of making the human rights situation known and even of reducing the number of serious abuses and violations of human rights in many countries.

> As no Committee is a Court with capacity to condemn anyone, it cannot be expected to impose sentences on States Parties which violate rights protected by an international instrument. But their decisions have virtually the same weight as passing a sentence, although no "international police" can force States to comply.

If a complaint has already been submitted to another legal body, a copy can still be sent to the corresponding Committee (as well as to any Special Rapporteur or Working Group which is studying the issue) so that it can take account of the actions when analysing the regular report of the State Party. In this case, it is appropriate to add a letter clarifying that the complaint is being submitted to such and such an authority and that copies are being sent for information only.

4) What can NGOs do?

Although according to the UN's Treaties it is the States Parties who must inform the Committees regarding fulfilment of these instruments in each country, NGOs (with or without consultative status) can access the treaty bodies and can make good use of them:

a) **on a national level**, by collaborating with governments in the drawing up of the periodic reports (a number of States have created mechanisms by which NGOs and individuals participate in this process; sometimes they also ask them to make comments on draft reports before submitting them). If national NGOs are not called upon to participate in the preparation and dissemination of the report and if they cannot gain access to it once it is ready, they should make this known to the members of the respective Committee;

b) **on an international level**, by carefully studying the periodic reports of the States Parties in order to submit well-founded criticisms on their content and to suggest comments or questions which could be made to government representatives when they are questioned by the Committee. They could also submit a "counter report" which refutes, completes or corrects the official report, highlighting what information should have been included by the government, which are the most serious problems in the country with regard to the rights covered by that instrument and recommending solutions. This material must be sent to the Office of the High Commissioner for Human Rights in sufficient time (some 4 months before the session in which the government report will be studied);

c) by commenting on, and publicly disseminating, both the observations made to the States Parties by the Treaty bodies as well as the commitments verbally assumed by the former, in order to put pressure on them;

d) by making known the fact that a State Party is not fulfilling its obligation to submit periodic reports on time;

e) by also publicly disseminating, as the case may be, the positive actions of States to strengthen the protection and promotion of human rights in territories under their jurisdiction. This type of declaration helps to gain the respect, confidence and support of some governments and may possibly lead to a greater acceptance regarding the idea of being examined by international bodies on the part of States.

f) as far as possible by sending representatives to public sessions of the Treaty bodies in order to give greater publicity to the procedure, to be aware of the responses of the government representatives, to have more complete and detailed information and to make personal contacts with the members of each Committee.

g) finally, by informing public opinion of the existence of international instruments for the protection of human rights and exercising greater pressure, at both a national and an international level, so that countries which have not yet either ratified or adhered to the existing Treaties may do so as soon as possible.

B. The International Bill of Human Rights

In its first work session, the Commission on Human Rights began to prepare the documents aimed at stating, defining and protecting the rights and fundamental freedoms of all human beings, regardless of race, sex, language or religion. **The Universal Declaration of Human Rights** was approved by the General Assembly of the United Nations on 10th December, 1948, a date which ever since has been known as International Human Rights Day. In this Declaration, a wide list of all the rights and fundamental freedoms recognised by the international community were proclaimed. In 1951, the General Assembly decided that in order to implement the Universal Declaration, it was necessary to draw up two Covenants, each one dealing with a specific category of rights: on the one hand, civil and political rights (the "classic" human rights); on the other hand, economic, social and cultural rights (the "new" human rights).

Civil and political rights guarantee the freedom, security and physical and spiritual integrity of people and can be immediately protected by States, simply through administrative, legal and judicial reforms, whilst **economic, social and cultural rights** refer to work and an adequate standard of living, health, education, culture and science, amongst other things, all of which require gradual measures and important investment on the part of States, something which poor countries are often not in a position to do rapidly. Thus the International Covenant on Economic, Social and Cultural Rights anticipates progressive application of economic and technical measures, in accordance with the resources which each State Party has at its disposal.

The main difference between the two International Covenants is thus the measures for implementation applicable to each one: immediate for one, gradual for the other. However both categories are considered indivisible and interdependent.

The International Covenant on Civil and Political Rights and the International Covenant on Economic, Social and Cultural Rights were approved by the General Assembly in 1966 and entered into force in 1976. Together with the Universal Declaration of Human Rights they make up the International **Bill of Human Rights** [see Fact Sheet No. 2 which includes the full text of the 3 instruments, and pages 4 to 7 of the booklet Human Rights. Questions and Answers: DPI/919].

The rights protected by these three instruments are considered so fundamental that there is an increasing tendency to treat them as obligatory commitments, even on the part of those States who have not ratified the Covenants. Several of them were subsequently developed in more depth within international instruments of a specific nature.

C. Six International Treaties on Human Rights

In this section we will present six international Treaties and their corresponding treaty bodies. These are instruments which we consider particularly relevant to the promotion and protection of the rights of indigenous peoples *[a more thorough list of existing instruments can be found in the publication United Nations Action in the Field of Human Rights and in Human Rights: a Compilation of International Instruments. See Bibliography]*.

SIX INTERNATIONAL TREATIES AND THEIR TREATY BODIES	
INTERNATIONAL TREATY	TREATY BODY
International Covenant on Civil and Political Rights	Human Rights Committee
International Covenant on Economic, Social and Cultural Rights	The Committee on Economic, Social and Cultural Rights
International Convention on the Elimination of all Forms of Racial Discrimination	Committee on the Elimination of Racial Discrimination
International Convention on the Elimination of all Forms of Discrimination against Women	Committee on the Elimination of Discrimination against Women
Convention on the Rights of the Child	Committee on the Rights of the Child
Convention against Torture and Other Cruel, Inhuman or Degrading Treatment or Punishment	Committee against Torture

1) The International Covenant on Civil and Political Rights; the Optional Protocol and the Human Rights Committee (CCPR)

- *The rights protected by the Covenant*

The International Covenant on Civil and Political Rights guarantees a series of rights to peoples and individuals aimed at protecting the freedom of the individual before the State (civil rights) and aimed at enabling his participation within the political structure of his or her society (political rights). Some of the rights which this Covenant recognises are:

- **for peoples**, the right to self-determination (defined as the right to freely determine their political status, to freely pursue their economic, social and cultural development and to freely dispose of their natural wealth and resources). The Covenant clarifies that "in no case may a people be deprived of its own means of subsistence" (Article 1, which is identical to Article 1 of the International Covenant on Economic, Social and Cultural Rights).
- **for individuals**, the right to freedom from discrimination, the right to life, to freedom from torture, slavery, servitude, forced or compulsory labour, the right to liberty and security of person, to be brought before a judge if arrested and to be entitled to recourse to justice and the legal system on the basis of equality, to enjoy legal guarantees (such as the right to have proceedings interpreted in a language which he or she understands), the right to freedom of movement and the freedom to choose one's place of residence, freedom of thought, conscience and religion, freedom to participate in the political life of the country (to elect and be elected to public office), etc.

Article 4 of the Covenant indicates the civil and political rights which, under certain conditions, can legitimately be suspended by the State Party in time of public emergency (exceptional public danger which threatens the existence of the nation). A group of essential rights makes up what are known as the **inalienable rights** of all human beings from which under no circumstances can there be derogation. This relates to the right to life, to recognition as a person before the law, to freedom of thought, conscience and religion, to freedom from torture, slavery or servitude, to freedom from imprisonment for debt and freedom from penalty for acts which did not constitute crimes at the moment of being committed.

Article 27 of the Covenant guarantees to **members of ethnic, religious or linguistic minorities** the right to enjoy "in community with the other members of their group", their "own culture, to profess and practice their own religion, or to use their own language". Although indigenous peoples are not "ethnic minorities" but peoples, they can enforce their cultural rights by calling upon this article. There is a famous precedent: the case of Sandra Lovelace, an indigenous Canadian woman who, in 1981, managed to recover her indigenous status which was being denied her by the State for having married a white person, and she was able to continue living with her people.

- *The Human Rights Committee*

In Article 28, the Covenant establishes the Human Rights Committee, which meets three times each year for three weeks at a time (in general, the July and November sessions are in Geneva, whilst the March session is in New York). The States Parties must submit an initial report in the year in which the Covenant enters into force in their country and, subsequently, every five years. The Committee also receives written information from the specialized agencies and numerous NGOs *[see Fact Sheet No. 15. The Human Rights Committee Rules of procedure can be found in document CCPR//3/Rev.1 (1979)].*

- *The submission of individual complaints under the Optional Protocol to the International Covenant on Civil and Political Rights*

The Covenant on Civil and Political Rights was completed with two Optional Protocols. Through the means of the first, the States Parties can recognise the competence of the Committee to receive communications from individuals who claim to be victims of a violation of their rights. As of 30th June, 1998, the first Optional Protocol had been ratified by 92 States.

Unlike the 1503 Procedure of the Commission on Human Rights *[see Chapter 1]*, the Optional Protocol's procedure does not permit NGOs or third persons to submit complaints regarding human rights violations unless acting as the authorised representatives of the victims or if the victims are unable to act on their own behalf. In this case, the author of the communication must prove their close connection with the victim.

A complaint submitted against a State Party to the Optional Protocol must indicate which right protected by the Covenant has been violated. You should previously ascertain that the State has imposed no reservation upon that article, because in this case the communication would not be admissible.

Communications must be sent to the Office of the High Commissioner for Human Rights of the United Nations, in Geneva, including any documentation which proves what happened and that recourse to internal justice has been exhausted (Fax: (4122) 917-9022). If the victim was unable to gain access to internal legal channels, if they were not effective or did not provide the necessary guarantees, statements demonstrating this must be included (reports from human rights organizations or statements from defence lawyers regarding the defects of the legal system in that country). The Human Rights Committee has prepared a model communication submitted under the Optional Protocol *[see Fact Sheet No. 7: 19-20].*

- *The Second Optional Protocol*

The Second Optional Protocol, approved in 1989, deals with abolition of the death penalty. As of 30th June, 1998 it had been ratified by 33 States.

2) The International Covenant on Economic, Social and Cultural Rights and the Committee on Economic, Social and Cultural Rights (CESCR)

- *The rights protected by the Covenant*

According to the Covenant on Economic, Social and Cultural Rights, these rights must be guaranteed to individuals by the State, which thus assumes a role of promotion of the economic and social well-being of all people within its jurisdiction. The States Parties commit themselves to implementing immediate measures which will progressively enable the full realisation of these rights, making maximum use of the resources available to them.

Like the Covenant on Civil and Political Rights, this Treaty recognises the right of peoples to self-determination, to the control and use of their natural wealth and resources and the right of individuals to freedom from discrimination of any kind (race, sex, language, religion), as well as the right of association and unionisation.

Besides these rights, which are common to both Covenants, it deals in particular with the rights of the individual to just and favourable working conditions, to social security, to a decent standard of living (that is, to adequate food, clothing and housing), to health, education (including free primary school), to participate in cultural life and scientific progress.

The Covenant makes no reference to the right to property, in particular the right to land, which is of exceptional importance to indi-genous peoples. The only international instruments which specifically protect the right of indigenous peoples to land are Convention Ns. 107 (Article 11) and 169 (Article 14) of the International Labour Organization *[see Chapter 4]*.

- *The Committee on Economic, Social and Cultural Rights*

Since the Covenant on Economic, Social and Cultural Rights did not provide for the creation of a supervisory body, in 1978 ECOSOC set up a Working Group to study periodic reports from the States Parties to the Covenant. In 1985, this Working Group became the Committee on Economic, Social and Cultural Rights. It holds two periods of session per year in Geneva, the first in the middle of May and the second in November/December. A Working Group made up of five members of the Committee meets six months prior to each session, for a preliminary reading of the reports which will be considered by the Committee and to detect any possible lack of information. On the basis of this, the Working Group draws up lists of questions to be submitted to the respective governments so that they may reply in writing prior to the session in which their report is to be considered *[see Fact Sheet No. 16 (Rev. 1), which includes the text of the Covenant]*.

- *The reports of the States Parties to the Covenant*

The principal means of implementation of the Covenant is the presentation of periodic reports (the first two years after entering into force, then every five years). To facilitate the presentation of reports, the Committee has drawn up guidelines indicating the sort of information which it considers relevant. The Committee maintains that, on ratifying the Covenant, each State Party has the immediate obligation of ensuring the satisfaction of at least a basic level of each of the rights recognised in the Covenant, even in times of serious limitation of resources. Vulnerable members of society, in particular, must be protected in these circumstances. The States Parties may take the opportunity of highlighting in their reports what their concrete needs for technical assistance or development cooperation are. The Committee may also provide assistance to the States Parties by formulating suggestions and recommendations of a legislative and political nature in order to promote the application of the measures of the Covenant in each country.

The Covenant does not provide for any complaints procedure regarding lack of fulfilment. In 1996, the Committee finalised the drafting of an Optional Protocol to establish a mechanism for submission of individual complaints and this is currently being considered by the Commission on Human Rights. Some specialized agencies of the United Nations (ILO, UNESCO, WHO, FAO) provide additional information to the Committee with regard to the areas of work which they cover. NGOs are also invited to submit written information to the Committee at any time and to make oral presentations during the Working Group meetings which are held between sessions. The secretariat of the Committee on Economic, Social and Cultural Rights can be reached by phone: (4122) 917-9321 or fax: (4122) 917-9022.

Once reports have been analysed and dialogue with the States Parties undertaken, the Committee writes up its final observations, which contain suggestions and recommendations to the States. On the basis of its annual report to ECOSOC, this latter may draw the attention of the General Assembly, or other competent organs, to situations of concern in any country. The reports of the Committee on Economic, Social and Cultural Rights are available at the Internet site of the Office of the UN High Commissioner for Human Rights [http://www.unhchr.ch].

3) International Convention on the Elimination of All Forms of Racial Discrimination and the Committee on the Elimination of Racial Discrimination (CERD)

In 1963, the General Assembly approved the International Convention on the Elimination of All Forms of Racial Discrimination, and the Sub-

Commission then immediately began to draft the text of the International Convention on the Elimination of All Forms of Racial Discrimination, which was adopted by the GA in 1965 and entered into force in 1969.

- *The rights protected by the Convention on the Elimination of Racial Discrimination*

The Convention describes **discrimination** as "any distinction, exclusion, restriction or preference based on race, colour, descent or national or ethnic origin which has the purpose or effect of nullitying or impairing the recognition, enjoyment or exercise, on an equal footing, of human rights and fundamental freedoms". Amongst other things, the Convention guarantees individuals the right to receive equal treatment before the law and to rely on effective means of recourse to national judicial authorities.

The States Parties must ban discriminatory practices and, if necessary, **give protection to certain particular groups** who may need it. They also commit themselves to legally prohibiting and punishing any act of discrimination and all propaganda or organizations who support theories based on racial or ethnic superiority. The States which ratify the Convention take on the responsibility of implementing immediate measures in the areas of education, culture and information in order to fight the prejudice which leads to racial discrimination, and to encourage a better understanding of, and tolerance between, racial and ethnic groups.

- *The Committee on the Elimination of Racial Discrimination*

The Committee on the Elimination of Racial Discrimination (known as CERD) began operating in 1969 and was the first organ dedicated to verifying the application of an international human rights Treaty. It meets twice a year in Geneva (usually in August and March).

The States Parties must present their **reports** on the year in which the Convention entered into force and subsequently every four years. The situation of indigenous peoples within their national borders are often mentioned in these reports, but **no indigenous people has yet used the mechanisms which the Convention puts at their disposal**. It is important to be aware that, in order to evaluate the periodic reports of the States Parties, the Committee's experts will receive any documentation on the existence of discriminatory practices based on racial prejudice as long as it is well-founded.

Since 1974, CERD has prepared a public summary of its analysis of each periodic report of the States Parties, including the opinions of the Committee and of its members. These summaries appear within CERD's annual report to the General Assembly and can be freely consulted *[see Fact Sheet No. 12 and Human Rights, Questions and Answers: 23-25]*.

- *The submission of individual complaints to CERD*

According to Article 14 of the Convention, any individual or group of individuals within the jurisdiction of a State Party which has recognised the competence of the Committee to receive this type of complaint may submit communications alleging a violation of any of the measures of the Convention on the part of that State or of individuals. The complaint is passed on confidentially to the State in question, without making known the identity of the plaintiff, unless he or she expressly authorises it. Once an explanation has been received from the State, CERD studies it and makes known its suggestions and recommendations, both to the plaintiff and to the State. CERD also receives regular information from the Trusteeship Council *[see Chapter 1]* and the Committee on Decolonization regarding the situation in colonial or Trust territories.

Countries which, in accordance with Article 14 of the Convention, have recognised the competence of the Committee to receive individual complaints up to December, 1998, are: Algeria, Australia, Bulgaria, Chile, Costa Rica, Cyprus, Denmark, Ecuador, Finland, France, Hungary, Iceland, Italy, Luxembourg, Norway, Netherlands (Holland), Peru, Republic of Korea, the Russian Federation, Senegal, Slovakia, Spain, Sweden, Ukraine and Uruguay.

Article 14 of the Convention also recommends that States Parties should create some form of national body to receive complaints from people who have exhausted recourse to other means.

> ARIS (Anti-Racism Information Service) is an NGO which distributes information on the Convention and on the work of the Committee on the Elimination of Racial Discrimination. It thus tries to facilitate access to CERD on the part of interested individuals and national organizations. All kinds of documentation can be sent to it, as well as copies of communications sent to the Committee, so that they can follow them up. ARIS also publishes a bulletin. Write to: ARIS (Anti-Racism Information Service), 14, Avenue Trembley, 1209 Geneva, Switzerland. Tel: (4122) 740-3530 and fax: (4122) 740-3565. Email: aris@geneve-link.ch.

4) The Convention on the Elimination of All Forms of Discrimination Against Women and the Committee on the Elimination of Discrimination Against Women (CEDAW)

The UN and its specialized agencies have dealt with the issue of discrimination against women right from the very start: in 1946 the

Commission on the Status of Women *[see Chapter 1]* was established and very soon it had drawn up a broad range of international legal standards to prevent and correct this practice. The most relevant of these are:
- the Convention on the Suppression of the Traffic in Persons and of the Exploitation of the Prostitution of Others (1949);
- ILO Convention No. 100 on equal remuneration for men and women workers for work of equal value (1951);
- Convention on the Political Rights of Women (1952);
- Convention on the Nationality of Married Women (1957);
- Convention on Consent to Marriage, Minimum Age for Marriage and Registration of Marriages (1962).

Finally, in 1967 the **Declaration on the Elimination of all Forms of Discrimination against Women** was proclaimed, which condemned all unfair discriminatory practices against women as contradictory to human dignity. On this basis, the respective Convention was drawn up and approved by the General Assembly in 1979.

- *The rights protected by the Convention on the Elimination of Discrimination against Women*

This instrument, which brings all the measures of the previous texts together in just one document, protects the civil, political, social, economic and family rights of women all over the world from discrimination due to reasons of gender. It also clarifies, amongst other things, that the traditional role of the man within the family, and in society in general, must evolve along with that of the woman in order to achieve true equality.

Article 14, which refers to **rural women**, is particularly important for indigenous women. This recognises the following rights: to participate in the elaboration and implementation of development planning for the rural sector; to health (including the right to family planning); to social security; to training and education; to the organization of self-help groups and cooperatives; to participate in all community activities; to have access to credit, marketing and appropriate technology services and to adequate living conditions *[see the text of the Convention in A Compilation of International Instruments and in Fact Sheet No. 22]*.

- *The Committee on the Elimination of Discrimination Against Women*

Article 17 created the **Committee on the Elimination of Discrimination Against Women (CEDAW)**, which has met once a year since 1982, for two weeks (usually at the end of January) in New York. There is a proposal pending approval that this should become two longer periods of session every year.

Three Working Groups help CEDAW in its task: the first, which meets before the period of session, prepares an analysis of the reports to be considered; the second and third sit in parallel with CEDAW and deal, respectively, with making suggestions to speed up the work of CEDAW and deepening the Convention's measures of implementation. In order to analyse the reports presented by the States Parties (initially after two years of the Convention entering into force and subsequently every four years), the Committee receives information from the specialized agencies of the UN, other governmental sources and non-governmental organizations.

To send information to CEDAW you can write via the Division for the Advancement of Women:

> 2 UN Plaza, DC 2 - 12th Floor,
> New York, NY 10017,
> Fax: (1 212) 963-3463
> Email: daw@un.org
> http://www-un.org/womenwatch/daw/csw

The Convention establishes no procedure for the submission of communications, although work is being done on an optional protocol which would provide for the possibility of submitting individual complaints. For the moment, CEDAW is limited to making general recommendations which are valid for all the States Parties.

> As of December 1996, 154 countries had ratified this Convention. In spite of such apparently massive acceptance, it is the instrument which has received the greatest number of reservations and interpretative declarations. According to members of the Committee and a number of States Parties, this may affect the full implementation of its measures.

---

5) The Convention on the Rights of the Child and the Committee on the Rights of the Child (CRC)

The United Nation's interest in children's rights was initially shown through the creation of UNICEF (the United Nations Children's Fund). In 1959, the Declaration on the Rights of the Child was proclaimed and thirty years later the Convention on the Rights of the Child. This entered into force in 1990 and was ratified by all States, with the exception of the United States of America and Somalia. The States Parties must submit their first report two years after having ratified the Convention, and subsequently every five years.

- *The rights protected by the Convention*

The Convention defines a child as "every human being below the age of 18 years of age unless, under the law applicable to the child, majority is attained earlier" (Article 1). It protects a wide range of civil, political, economic, social and cultural rights and prohibits all kinds of child exploitation (economic, sexual), as well as the recruitment of children under fifteen years of age as soldiers in situations of conflict *[see Fact Sheet No. 10 (Rev 1)]*.

Of particular importance to **indigenous children** are Article 5, which is a commitment to respect "the responsibilities, **rights and duties of parents** or, where applicable, the members of the extended family or community as provided for by local custom..."; Article 17, which guarantees the **right of access to information**, having "particular regard to the linguistic needs of the child who belongs to a minority group or who is indigenous"; Article 20, which provides for special protection and assistance for **children deprived of their family environment**, considering the desirability of "continuity in a child's upbringing" and taking into account "the child's ethnic, religious, cultural and linguistic background"; Article 29, which establishes that the **education** of the child must be directed towards development of respect "for his or her own cultural identity, language and values" and Article 30 which protects the right of children belonging to ethnic, religious or linguistic minorities and to children of indigenous origin to enjoy their own **culture**, to profess and practice their own religion and to use their own language "in common with the other members of their group".

Since 1994, a Working Group has been working on a **draft Optional Protocol on the participation of children in situations of armed conflict**, with the aim of raising the age at which children can be enlisted as soldiers from 15 to 18 years. Some States (United States of America, Kuwait, Korea and Israel) are opposed to setting the minimum age at 18, whilst others oppose having to amend their national legislation to adapt to international standards. This is delaying the process of approval of this Protocol. Another Working Group should conclude a **draft Optional Protocol on the sale of children, prostitution and child pornography** by the year 2000.

- *The Committee on the Rights of the Child*

The Committee on the Rights of the Child has competence to study periodic reports from States Parties, to make general recommendations and suggestions and to propose studies on questions relating to children's rights.

It meets three times per year in Geneva, for four weeks each time, in January, May/June and September/October. Two months prior to each period of session (in November, February/March and June/July) a preparatory Working Group meets which, on the basis of a summary drawn up by the Office of the High Commissioner for Human Rights, studies the information received from different sources on each country to be studied. Governments, other conventional bodies, specialized agencies of the UN system, specialized mechanisms of the Commission on Human Rights and NGOs can provide any information which they consider relevant to the work of the Committee.

> The afternoon of the first day of work of this Working Group is always devoted to **listening to the NGOs present** which wish to speak on the situation of children in the countries in question. Each NGO has around ten minutes in which to speak and can leave written documentation with the members of the Working Group which complements what has been verbally discussed.

Once its analysis of each government's report has been completed, the CRC adopts final observations regarding ways in which fulfilment of the measures of the Treaty could be improved in that country. These observations should be widely diffused at a national level, with the aims of promoting public debate defining the problems and discussing appropriate means of resolving them. The Committee submits a report to ECOSOC every two years, although it writes a report after each of its sessions.

In collaboration with UNICEF, it holds annual **meetings in particular places**, visiting a different region each time. On these occasions, the members of the Committee dialogue directly with national and regional authorities, as well as with NGOs and individuals who wish to meet them to provide information. Each year, in the September/October session of the Committee, a day of general discussion is also held on a theme of interest, which may be proposed by a member of the Committee, a specialized agency or an NGO.

The Convention provides for **no mechanism for the submission of communications**, but in situations where serious violations of the rights of the child are noted, recourse may be made to the specialized mechanisms of the Commission on Human Rights which deals with these rights *[see Chapter 2]*.

In1983, a number of NGOs concerned with the rights of the child formed a Group to promote the elaboration of a Convention and other international standards aimed at protecting children's rights. Once the Convention on the Rights of the Child was approved, they continued to work on its implementation and follow up. Amongst these NGOs, who work in close collaboration with the Committee on the Rights of the Child, are **Defence for Children International, Rädda Barnen** ("Save the Children") and **Anti-Slavery International**.

> National and regional NGOs are recommended to contact the Secretariat of Defence for Children International in Geneva for information regarding the Committee on the Rights of the Child and the work of the NGO Group for the Convention on the Rights of the Child, as well as on regional coordination efforts. For more information, write to:
> 1, rue de Varembé,
> PO Box 88, 1211, Geneva 20,
> Tel: (4122) 734-0558- Fax (4122) 740-1145
> e-mail: dci-hq@pingnet.ch
> Internet: http//www.childhub.ch/ebpub/dcihome

6) The Convention against Torture and the Committee against Torture (CAT)

In the 1970s, the United Nations began to draw up a series of standards to combat the practice of torture. In 1971, the Standard Minimum Rules for the Treatment of Prisoners was approved, which proposed suitable methods for the treatment of prisoners and the management of penal institutions. In 1975, the Declaration on the Protection of All Personas from Being Subjected to Torture and Other Cruel, Inhuman or Degrading Treatment or Punishment was proclaimed. In 1979, the Code of Conduct for Law Enforcement Officials was drawn up, which strictly forbids public officials to resort to torture; in 1982, the Principles of Medical Ethics, which considers the participation of health staff in acts of torture a crime; and finally, in 1984, the Convention against Torture and other Cruel, Inhuman or Degrading Treatment or Punishment, which entered into force in 1987 [see Fact Sheet No. 4].

- *The right to protection from torture*

In Article 1, the Convention defines **torture** as "any act by which severe pain or suffering, whether physical or mental, is intentionally inflicted on a person, for such purposes as obtaining from him or a third person, information or a confession, punishing him for an act he or a third person has committed or is suspected of having committed, or intimidating or coercing him or a third person, or for any reason based on discrimination of any kind". These acts only constitute torture if they are committed, ordered or tolerated by a public official or someone acting in an official capacity.

In the following articles, the Convention details the obligations **which the States Parties must assume** in order to fight against torture, be it through adopting legislative, administrative, judicial or other measures in each country, or ensuring that no person is expelled from their territory if they may be tortured in the country of destination. Any participation, complicity or attempts to commit torture must be punished. As protection from torture is an inalienable right from which there is no derogation *[see comments to Article 4 of the International Covenant on Civil and Political Rights]*, under no circumstances can acts of torture be justified, neither by exceptional circumstances nor by the law of "due obedience" *[the text of the Convention against Torture can be found in the annex to Fact Sheet No. 17]*.

- *The Committee against Torture*

The Committee against Torture (CAT) meets twice per year in Geneva, during the last two weeks of April and November. In order to **study government reports** (the first in the year in which the Convention enters into force in each State and then subsequently every four years), the CAT invites specialized agencies, the interested UN organs, regional intergovernmental organizations and NGOs to provide it with additional information. It is a good opportunity to note whether measures adopted in national legislation are being fulfilled in practice or not. *[see Fact Sheet No. 17]*.

The CAT also submits an **annual activity report** to the States Parties and to the General Assembly. If it receives information indicating that torture is being systematically practised in a particular country, the Committee may invite the State Party to cooperate in an examination of the information received and to make observations. If the case merits it, the Committee may also **commence a confidential investigation**, requesting the collaboration of the State Party. The investigation may include a visit to its territory (Article 20).

As of 5th December, 1997, 104 States had ratified or adhered to the Convention against Torture, whilst another 11 had signed it only.

- *The submission of complaints of torture to the CAT*

In Article 22, the Convention establishes the procedure for receiving **communications from individuals** who are the victims of torture, as long as the States Parties recognise the competence of the Committee to do so. As of 5th December, 1997, 39 States Parties to the Convention had made the declaration provided for in Article 22. They are Algeria, Argentina, Australia, Austria, Bulgaria, Canada, Croatia, Cyprus, Czech Republic, Denmark, Ecuador, Finland, France, Greece, Hungary, Iceland, Italy, Liechtenstein, Luxembourg, Malta, Monaco, the Netherlands, New Zealand, Norway, Poland, Portugal, the Russian Federation, Senegal,

Slovakia, Slovenia, Spain, Sweden, Switzerland, Togo, Tunisia, Turkey, Uruguay, Venezuela and Yugoslavia. The requirements for admissibility of these communications and the procedure to be followed are the same as those for the Optional Protocol of the Convention on Civil and Political Rights and the Convention on Racial Discrimination outlined earlier *[see the form for the submission of communications in Fact Sheet No. 17]*.

It is important to be aware that, in the case of torture or the imminent danger of someone being tortured, the Committee against Torture is not very effective, because its procedures are slow. You should contact the Special Rapporteur of the Commission on Human Rights, who can act rapidly by intervening with any government, whether they have ratified the Convention against Torture or not *[see Chapter 2]*.

Amongst the NGOs which actively collaborate in the work of the CAT are Amnesty International, SOS-Torture, the International Commission of Jurists and Americas Watch.

- *The draft Optional Protocol to the Convention against Torture*

An ad-hoc Working Group is currently drafting an Optional Protocol with the aim of creating a **preventive system of regular visits to detention centres** at an international level (without the need for authorisation from the State Party), such as already exists on a European level. This would enable the detection and correction of the causes and conditions which are at the root of the problem of torture in order to prevent cases of torture and ill treatment from occurring.

The following table summarises some of the practical information on the six bodies which we have just provided:

NAME	DATE	PLACE	COMPLAINTS	LEAFLET N°
CCPR	March, July and November	Geneva/ New York	Yes, if the country has ratified the Optional Protocol	7 and 15
CESCR	April/ May and November/ December	Geneva	No	16 (Rev. 1)
CERD	March and August	Geneva	Yes, according to Art. 14 of the Convention	12
CEDAW	January/February and June/July	New York	No	22
CRC	January, May/June and September/ October	Geneva	No	10 (Rev. 1)
CAT	May, November	Geneva	Yes, according to Article 22	4 and 17

D. Other International Instruments of Relevance

The following instruments protect essential collective rights, but do not always provide for a supervisory mechanism to control government action in this respect. This lack of such a mechanism severely limits their effectiveness.

1) The Convention against Genocide and the International Criminal Court

In 1948, with the horrors of Nazi Germany fresh in its mind, the General Assembly proclaimed the Convention on the Prevention and Punishment of the Crime of Genocide, which entered into force in 1951. In its text it defines **genocide** as the methodical extermination of an ethnic, national, racial or religious group and establishes it as a crime under international law, whether it is committed during times of peace or times of war. This means that, by establishing it as a crime against the moral rules of all societies it is considered as a **"crime against humanity"**, which all States should avoid and punish, whether or not they are Parties to this Convention.

In 1968 the Convention was complemented by the Convention on the Non-Applicability of Statutory Limitations to War Crimes and Crimes Against Humanity (which entered into force in 1970). This established that for crimes such as genocide and *apartheid* no statutory date would apply irrespective of the date of their commission (this means that the guilty parties may be brought before the relevant Court at any time).

- *The crime of genocide*

Article 2 describes the group of actions which constitute the crime of genocide:
    a) killing members of the group;
    b) causing serious bodily or mental harm to members of the group;
    c) deliberately inflicting on the group conditions of life calculated to bring about its physical destruction, in whole or in part;
    d) imposing measures intended to prevent births within the group;
    e) forcibly transferring children of the group to another group.

The Convention punishes both genocide and conspiracy to commit, incitement to commit, attempts to commit and complicity in genocide (Article 3).

- *Implementation of the Convention against Genocide*

The mechanisms for implementation provided for this Convention are the effective **legislative measures** and **criminal punishments** of the

States Parties against those guilty of this crime. Although no control body has been created to supervise its regulations, the Convention anticipates that the States Parties may call upon "the competent organs of the UN" (including the International Court of Justice) in order to take appropriate measures. Since 1948 discussions have taken place on the possibility of creating an International Criminal Court to judge those responsible for this serious crime. It is only 50 years later that this project may come true.

In practice, for several decades the Commission on Human Rights and its Sub-Commission have regularly received individual complaints of genocide, referring in particular to indigenous peoples. In order to deepen its study of the issue, the Sub-Commission appointed a Special Rapporteur on Genocide in 1983, who looked into the systematic massacres of the Aché (Guayaki) Indians of Paraguay.

- *The establishment of a permanent International Criminal Court*

The brutal massacres which took place in ex-Yugoslavia and Rwanda during the 1990s, accompanied by a long series of other serious violations of human rights and humanitarian law, gave new impetus to the idea of establishing a higher international legal body to judge those responsible for crimes against humanity. As a first measure, the Security Council established, in 1993 and 1994 respectively, ad-hoc International Criminal Tribunals for ex-Yugoslavia and Rwanda, giving them the mandate of monitoring respect for the regulations of international criminal law and international humanitarian law, and of criminally indicting those assumed responsible for the serious violations of those rights which took place during both conflicts. The work of these two ad-hoc tribunals was an important step towards the elaboration of the Statute of the International Criminal Court, finally adopted in Rome on 17th July, 1998 [*doc. A/CONF/183/C/1/L.76, Adds. 1-14. The text of the Statute may also be consulted via the Internet at the following web site: http://www.un.org/icc*].

The Statute establishes an independent and permanent International Criminal Court, linked to the United Nations System, whose actions will be complementary to those of national criminal jurisdictions. This means that it will only act in cases where States are not exercising their own jurisdiction, be it through inability or lack of will to do so. This assumes that States cannot avoid their responsibility to investigate and try cases: when they do not do so, a complementary jurisdiction will exist to seek for justice and avoid impunity of those responsible of the most serious human rights violations .

The Court will function on a permanent basis with its seat established in The Hague (Netherlands) and it will be able to exercise its jurisdiction and powers within the territory of all States Parties to the Statute.

The International Criminal Court will be competent to try those responsible for the most serious crimes of concern to the international community as a whole. This mandate includes the following crimes: genocide, crimes against humanity, war crimes and crimes of aggression.

The Statute reiterates the definition of genocide adopted by the Convention against Genocide but leaves the definition of crimes of aggression for a future date, a task to be carried out by the States Parties to the Statute, through a reform of the same. On the other hand, it gives exhaustive definitions of the other two crimes included under the jurisdiction of the Court. According to the text, crimes against humanity exist when the following acts are noted, committed as part of a massive or systematic attack against any civilian population, in full awareness of the attack:

1) Murder;
2) Extermination;
3) Enslavement;
4) Deportation or forced transfer of population;
5) Imprisonment or other severe deprivation of physical liberty in violation of the fundamental rules of international law;
6) Torture;
7) Rape, sexual slavery, enforced prostitution, forced pregnancy, enforced sterilisation, or any other form of sexual violence of comparable gravity;
8) Persecution against any identifiable group or collectivity on political, racial, national, ethnic, cultural, religious, gender, or other grounds that are universally recognisable as inadmissible under international law;
9) Enforced disappearance of persons;
10) The crime of apartheid;
11) Other inhuman acts of a similar character intentionally causing great suffering, or serious injury to body or to mental or physical health.

Thus, as opposed to the crime of genocide, crimes against humanity include those crimes which are caused as a consequence of persecution on political, cultural or gender grounds, as well as crimes committed against the civilian population by parties to an armed conflict which is not of an international nature.

With regard to war crimes, these include:
1) Grave breaches of the Geneva Conventions of 1949 (the basis of international humanitarian law, which particularly protects the

non-combatant population, be they civilians, humanitarian personnel or troops outside of the field of combat for whatever reason). These violations refer, in particular and amongst other acts, to wilful killing, torture or inhuman treatment (including biological experiments), wilfully causing great suffering or serious injury to body or health, extensive destruction and appropriation of property not justified by military necessity and carried out unlawfully and wantonly, etc.
2) Other serious violations of the laws and customs applicable in armed conflict, such as intentionally directing attacks against the civilian population, against non-military targets, against installations, material or personnel involved in humanitarian assistance, amongst many other acts of war.
3) In the case of internal armed conflict, cruel acts against those taking no active part in the hostilities, in violation of the Geneva agreements of 1949 (violence, murder, mutilation, cruel treatment and torture, outrages on personal dignity, taking of hostages and the passing of sentences or carrying out of executions without judgement by the appropriate Court). Internal disturbances and isolated and internal sporadic disturbances are excluded from the definition of armed conflict.

Through Article 12 of the Statute, the States Parties accept the jurisdiction of the Court in respect of the crimes mentioned. The International Criminal Court may exercise its jurisdiction at the request of a State Party, the Security Council or when the Prosecutor himself initiates an investigation about the crimes mentioned. In all cases, the Security Council has the authority (Article 16) to defer the commencement or continuation of an investigation or trial against a State Party for a period of twelve months.

Although this attribute of the Security Council constitutes a considerable limitation to the powers of the International Criminal Court, the adoption of the Statute of the ICC is a great step forward in the process of establishing an international body to monitor the effective application of the rules of international law. Its capacity to punish individuals responsible for the most serious human rights violations is a valuable contribution in the fight against impunity. The powers given to the Prosecutor to initiate court-appointed investigations and the possibility for victims to participate in the reparations stage are significant advances towards the democratisation of investigations. Finally, the permanent nature of the International Criminal Court gives a greater guarantee of egalitarian treatment of States, large or small, weak or strong, than did the ad-hoc tribunals, which have been set up for some States only.

2) The Declaration on the Granting of Independence to Colonial Countries and Peoples and the Committee on Decolonization

In 1960 the General Assembly recognised the right of colonial peoples to self-determination by adopting the Declaration on the Granting of Independence to Colonial Countries and Peoples, also known as **Resolution 1514 (XV)**.

According to this Declaration, which gave rise to international recognition of the independence of a large number of African and Asian countries from the 1960s onwards, "the principle of equal rights and self-determination of all peoples" is so fundamental that universal and effective respect for human rights and fundamental freedoms depends on it, as well as peaceful and friendly relations between peoples.

The Declaration contains the first formulation of the right of self-determination as we later find it in the two International Covenants on Human Rights: **the self-determination of peoples consists of the right to freely determine their political status, to freely pursue their economic, social and cultural development and to freely dispose of their natural wealth and resources**.

But this same document contains two other elements which limit the scope of this right: firstly, the use of the word "peoples", which seems to refer exclusively to inhabitants of non-European territories under colonial domination; secondly, the absolute protection of territorial integrity and the unity of existing States against any secessionist attempts. This means that, according to this instrument, only the inhabitants of territories which, in 1960, were still colonies (regardless of their ethnic composition and of whether they constituted a homogeneous "nation" or not) had the right to self-determination and could enforce that right by creating new independent States. The Declaration would not therefore be applied to colonised peoples living within independent States, as is the case of the majority of indigenous peoples.

Furthermore, the new States which emerged from this process of decolonisation would immediately receive guarantees that their "territorial integrity" would not be affected, even though serious internal conflicts motivated by a lack of ethnic or "national" cohesion within the new countries may persist.

As we saw earlier in this chapter, the two International Covenants on Human Rights proclaimed in 1966 took up this same definition of "self-determination", but converted it into a fundamental human right for all peoples, colonial or not.

- *The Special Committee on Decolonization*

In 1961, the General Assembly created the Special Committee to supervise the application of the Declaration on the Granting of Independence to Colonial Countries and Peoples, better known as the **Special Committee of 24** (although since 1980 it has been made up of 25 Member States). This Special Committee meets for several months of the year (March through to August) in New York, inviting colonial powers and national liberation movements to participate in its work.

Its mandate consists of **examining the application of the Declaration** in the territories considered colonial (taking into account political, constitutional, economic, social and educational aspects). The Committee **proposes concrete measures** on how to improve the application of the Declaration, **presents recommendations** to the General Assembly and **informs the Security Council of the United Nations** regarding events in those territories which may constitute a threat to world peace. The Special Committee may also **send missions** to those territories. The visits serve to obtain first hand information, ensure that the UN is present whilst the process of decolonisation is being prepared and as an observer during the last stages of the process (supervising elections and plebiscites, for example).

The Special Committee **receives communications from individuals or groups** concerned with the situation in territories which appear on the list drawn up by the Committee.

3) The Declaration on the Rights of People to Peace

Indigenous peoples are the frequent victims of violence, whether whilst defending their rights or finding themselves involuntarily in the middle of conflicts which are totally foreign to them. Their aspiration to live in peace is all the more heartfelt in as far as they are suffering the horrors of war in their own flesh.

The Declaration on the Rights of People to Peace, approved by the General Assembly in 1984, shows the desire to **eradicate war** from the life of humanity and **to avert a nuclear catastrophe**. Recognising that each State has the duty to ensure the peaceful life of its peoples, the Declaration proclaims the sacred right of peoples to peace, notes the obligation of each State to maintain this right and to promote its achievement and underlines that it is essential that State policies move towards the elimination of the threat of war. To do this it encourages **renouncing the use of force** in international relations and the peaceful resolution of international conflicts.

4) The Declaration on the Right to Development

Adopted by the General Assembly in 1986, this Declaration states that **development** is "a comprehensive economic, social, cultural and political process which aims at the constant improvement of the well-being of the entire population and of all individuals on the basis of their active, free and meaningful participation in development and in the fair distribution of benefits resulting therefrom".

The Declaration notes that the denial of civil, political, economic, social and cultural rights constitutes a worrying obstacle to development and that there is a close relationship between disarmament and development. Thus, resources freed up through disarmament measures should be dedicated to economic and social development and to the well-being of all peoples.

The Declaration asserts that States have the responsibility of creating favourable national and international conditions for the achievement of the human right to development. In this sense, they must take the necessary measures **to ensure equality of opportunity for all in their access** to basic resources, education, health services, food, housing, employment and in the fair distribution of income. The Declaration also invites States to guarantee the participation of women and the population as a whole in the development process.

CHAPTER 4

THE SPECIALIZED AGENCIES OF THE UNITED NATIONS AND INDIGENOUS PEOPLES

The United Nations has incorporated or created institutions which deal with issues linked to international cooperation for peace and development. These institutions may be **autonomous organizations**, **funds** or **special programmes** of the United Nations. They are called **"specialized agencies"**.

Some agencies elaborate standars for the protection of certain human rights and establish mechanisms to supervise the fulfilment of these standards on the part of States. Such is the case, for example, of the International Labour Organization (ILO) and the United Nations Educational, Scientific and Cultural Organization (UNESCO). Others promote human rights (especially economic, social and cultural rights) through technical and financial assistance to the developing world and to some particularly marginalized social categories, including indigenous peoples.

In this chapter, we have chosen a small number of specialized agencies which carry out activities of relevance to indigenous peoples. We give a short explanation of the structure and objectives of each institution and we indicate their standard-setting activities and the kind of technical and financial assistance they to provide indigenous peoples.

1. The International Labour Organization (ILO)

- *Its objectives and structure*

The ILO was established in 1919 with the aims of improving working conditions, assuring freedom of expression and of association and combating poverty in the world. **Social justice** was one of its founding principles. It is achieved when human beings live in conditions of freedom, dignity and economic security, with equality of opportunity, regardless of ethnic origin, religion or sex.

In 1946, the International Labour Organization became the first specialized agency of the UN.

This is the only international organization in which the most important social sectors of the working world are represented alongside governments: employers and workers. For this reason, the principal organs of the ILO have a **tripartite structure**.

The International Labour Organization is made up of:

- the **International Labour Conference**, composed of all Member States which have accepted the obligations of the ILO's Constitution[1]. Each Member State is represented by four delegates: two for the government, one for the employers and one for the workers. The International Labour Conference meets annually in Geneva in June and adopts or revises conventions and recommendations.

- the **Governing Body**, made up of 56 people (28 government representatives, 14 employer delegates and 14 worker delegates). The Governing Body draws up the agenda for the Conference and is responsible for the technical preparations and necessary consultations before the adoption of a convention or recommendation.

- the **International Labour Office** answers to the Governing Body and deals with the collection and distribution of information about regulations governing living and working conditions in the different countries. The Governing Body appoints the Director-General of the ILO. The International Labour Organization's headquarters is in Geneva (Switzerland).

- *The ILO and human rights*

The ILO has established standards for a number of fundamental human rights with the aim of improving the labour conditions and living standards of workers: the length of the working day and week; conditions of employment; working hours; an adequate minimum living wage; occupational health and safety; the prohibition of child labour and forced labour; the protection of women, the elderly and disabled; social security and the fight against unemployment; the freedom to unionise and the right to form professional associations, amongst other things.

Since its establishment, the ILO has passed some 350 conventions and recommendations on labour related issues.

Conventions lay down minimum standards to ensure respect for certain fundamental human rights. Once they have ratified them, the ILO's Member States become obliged to fulfil their provisions and to provide information regarding the measures taken to implement them.

Recommendations are measures proposed to Member States in order to guide them in the adoption or modification of their legislation and their practices in relation to certain issues. They are normally far more detailed than conventions but are not subject to ratification and there is thus no obligation to fulfil them.

> The texts of the standards approved by the ILO are available in Spanish, French and English on a single CD-ROM: ILOLEX on CD-ROM, a database which, along with the Constitution of the ILO, includes the reports of the Committee on Freedom of Association (since 1985), the observations of the Committee of Experts on the Application of Conventions and Recommendations (since 1987), the annual reports of the Commission on Application of the International Labour Conference (since 1987), the reports of the committees and commissions established to deal with representations and complaints made with respect to articles 24 and 26 of the ILO Constitution (reports published since 1985), as well as a list of ratifications by convention and by country. To order this CD, contact the Publications Office (PUB/VENTE) in Geneva: Tel: (41 22) 799-7301; fax (41 22) 799-6938; email pubvente@ilo.org. It can also be consulted directly via Internet: http://ilolex.ilo.ch:1567/public/.

- *Supervision of ILO conventions*

The most currently used supervisory mechanism is the **presentation of periodic reports** by the States Parties. The ILO Constitution also provides mechanisms for the **submission of complaints** regarding lack of fulfilment of the clauses of the international labour conventions.

a. Presentation and analysis of periodic reports

In their reports, the States Parties to each convention must describe the relevant national legislation and explain how this is applied in practice. Reports are prepared every two or four years, to be submitted to the **Committee of Experts on the Application of Conventions and Recommendations**. This Committee is made up of 18 independent experts who meet once a year in private session in order to examine the information received.

> The Committee of Experts also receives written comments from the employers' and workers' organizations in the respective country, from other organs of the ILO and from NGOs in consultative status with the ILO, which complement and correct the government information. These comments may be sent to the Committee at any time.

The employers' and workers' organizations' comments, as well as those from NGOs in consultative status with the ILO, are sent to the relevant government so that it may present its written observations. If the Committee of Experts suspects that a State Party is not fulfilling the provisions of a convention, it may request an additionalreport to be submitted earlier than anticipated by the said Convention.

When the Committee comes to the conclusion that a State is violating the clauses of a convention, it can respond in one of two ways: either by sending a **"direct request"** to the government and employer and worker organizations of that country to provide the required information or to take the necessary measures to fulfil the convention, or by making **"observations"** regarding the situation in the country, which are sent to the government and published in the Committee's annual report. This latter type of action is reserved for the most serious and persistent cases, when direct requests are less frequently used.

The report of the Committee of Experts is subsequently analysed by the **Conference Committee on the Application of Conventions and Recommendations**, established each year by the International Labour Conference. This Committee selects the most serious cases mentioned by the Committee of Experts and analyses them in depth. In urgent cases, it may deal with situations not mentioned in the Committee of Expert's report.

The Conference Committee organises **hearings** with government members in order to request explanations. It then presents a **written report** to the International Labour Conference regarding the difficulties the governments have in implementing the work conventions they have ratified. **A list of "serious or persistent" violations** is included in this report, which is published in the Minutes of the International Labour Conference.

When a government does not succeed in fulfilling the conventions it has ratified, it may request the help of the International Labour Office to establish **direct contacts**. The ILO appoints an official or an expert to visit the country, meet with the authorities and discuss the best way of solving the problems with them. This type of contact may also be initiated by the ILO itself, with the consent of the government.

b. The submission of complaints

The International Labour Organization has created four procedures for reporting non-compliance with labour conventions or with the basic principles of the organization. Two of them are described in the ILO's Constitution whilst two of them were created more recently. Complaints, accompanied by all the available supporting documentation, must always be sent to the Director-General of the ILO, who passes them on to the relevant body.

The address to which complaints should be sent is: Director-General of the ILO, 4 route des Morillons, 1211 Geneva 22. Tel (41 22) 799-6111. Fax (41 22) 798-8685.

SUPERVISORY MECHANISMS OF THE ILO CONVENTIONS

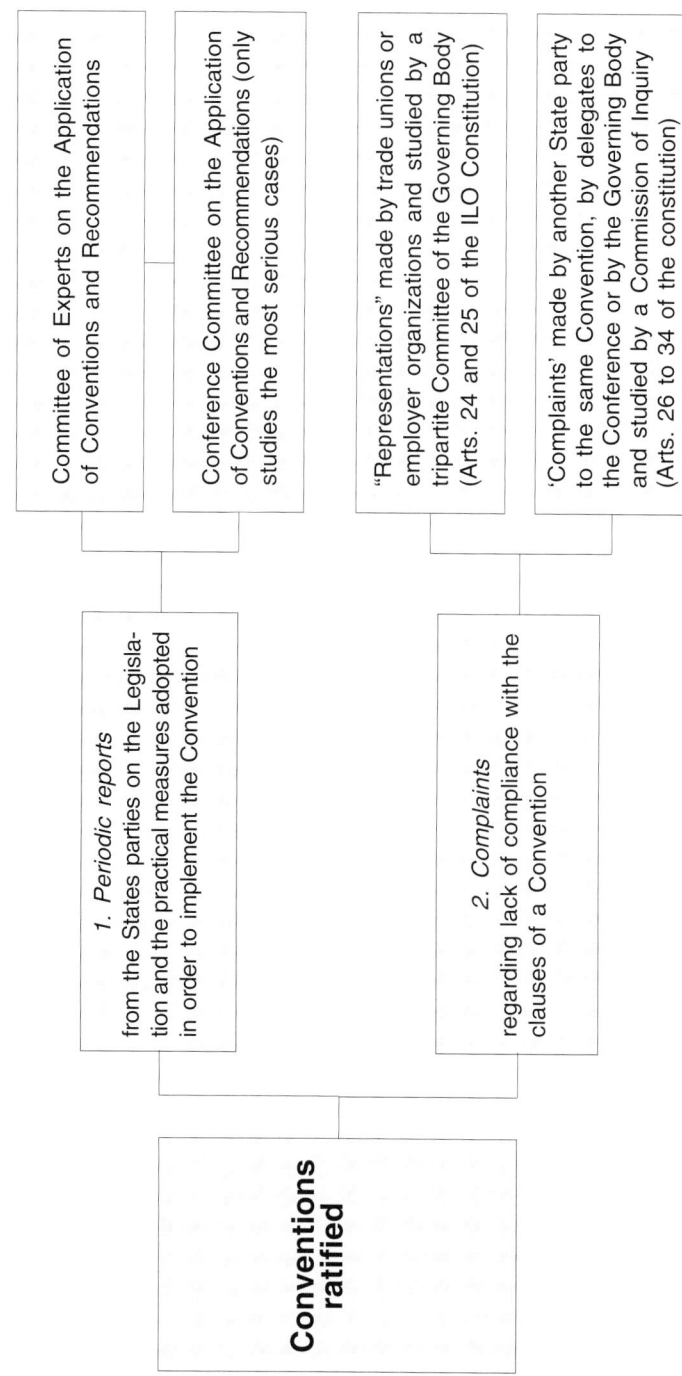

The procedures established by the ILO for the submission of complaints are the following:

1) The mechanism established in articles 24 and 25 of the Constitution for **complaints made by trade unions or employer organizations** (local, national or international) regarding non-compliance with the provisions of a convention by a State Party. These complaints are called **"representations"**. If the organization making the complaint is not well known internationally, it should add information regarding its composition and regulations.

The **Governing Body** of the ILO appoints a **Tripartite Committee** to study the representation and decide whether it should be transmitted to the State in question, a certain period of time being allowed in which to present its comments. With all this information, the Committee prepares its recommendations for the Governing Body which decides if the government is violating the measures of the convention or not.

If the government's replies to the Tripartite Committee are not satisfactory, the Governing Body may decide to **publish** the complaint, the government's reply and its own comments regarding the case, stating that the State is violating the provisions of an ILO convention. The situation of this country is then regularly monitored by two bodies which examine the periodic reports of the States Parties: the Committee of Experts and the Conference Committee on the Application of Conventions and Recommendations.

2) The mechanism provided for in articles 26 to 34 of the ILO Constitution for **complaints made by a State Party to a convention against another State Party** that it is not complying with the measures of that same convention. This procedure may also be initiated by any of the delegates to the International Labour Conference (government, worker or employer representatives) or by the ILO's Governing Body itself. In this way, the Governing Body is able to transform a "representation" submitted in accordance with article 24 into a "complaint", which may be taken further.

> The Director-General of the ILO submits each complaint he receives to the Governing Body. If this body considers it well-founded, it transmits it to the government in question, requesting its comments, and establishing a **Commission of Inquiry** which may request further written information from the plaintiff, the State or from business, union or non-governmental organizations interested in the case. The information thus collected is generally transmitted to all the other parties. The Commission of Inquiry may then carry out **hearings** in the ILO's offices, in which representatives of the parties and witnesses participate, or may send a **mission to the country**.

Once sufficient evidence has been gathered, the Commission of Inquiry comes to **conclusions** and makes **recommendations** which are binding on the part of the State, although if this latter is not in agreement it has the right to appeal to the International Court of Justice. The Commission also prepares a **report** for the Governing Body, published in the Official Bulletin of the ILO. It serves as a reference for the two organs responsible for supervising the application of the conventions and recommendations when they examine the country reports.

3) **Complaints regarding violations of the freedom of association**, which are presented to the **Committee on Freedom of Association**. This tripartite Committee is made up of nine members of the Governing Body and meets three times every year. It has competence regarding any violation of the freedom of association committed by a Member State, whether it has ratified the respective convention or not, since it relates to a fundamental principle enshrined in the ILO's Constitution.

> **The freedom of association** includes rights such as that of establishing professional associations, joining federations, confederations and international union organizations, that of collective bargaining and of striking, amongst others.

Any Member State, employer or worker organization or organization in consultative status with the ILO may submit written complaints. The Committee on Freedom of Association requests the State to comment within a given period of time. The Committee may request further information from the plaintiff and verbally question government representatives during the annual meetings of the Conference or carry out a direct contact mission in order to investigate the facts and enable an amicable solution to the conflict.

If it considers that the State is violating the right to freedom of association, the **Committee presents a full report** and **recommendations** which involve both the government and union organizations. The Committee may also ask the government to keep it informed regarding the application of the right of association in the country or, exceptionally, **refer the case to the Fact-finding and Conciliation Commission on Freedom of Association**.

This Commission, made up of independent experts appointed by the Governing Body, requests written information from the parties, organises hearings in Geneva and may carry out missions to investigate serious complaints and enter into conciliation negotiations.

> The Fact-finding and Conciliation Commission submits a report to the Governing Body including its conclusions and recommendations. These are not of a binding nature but the Committee on Freedom of Association may keep the situation under observation in the country.

4) The mechanism for **complaints regarding discriminatory employment practices**, set up in 1974, which may only be used by States, trade unions, employer organizations and NGOs in consultative status. Complaints must refer to discriminatory situations where, by virtue of race, colour, sex, religion, political opinion, nationality or social origin, a distinction or preference is made which affects equality of opportunity or treatment in the job or occupation.

5) Complaints are studied by the Governing Body's **Committee on Discrimination**. This organ is composed in a similar manner to the Committee on Freedom of Association. Complaints may be submitted against any Member State of the ILO, whether they have ratified the relevant Convention (No. 111) or not. If the situation merits it, the Committee requests the States authorisation to appoint a group of experts which will carry out a special study. Otherwise, it draws up a report for the Governing Body including its recommendations.

- *The ILO and indigenous peoples*

Since its creation, the ILO has studied the living and working conditions of indigenous and tribal peoples, who are generally reduced to situations of extreme poverty by the constant erosion of their territorial rights, discrimination in the labour market and the practice of forced labour to which they are frequently subjected. In 1930, **Convention No. 29 on Forced Labour** was adopted which, although not referring exclusively to indigenous peoples, did constitute a first instrument for their protection from exploitation. In 1953, a book was published, "Indigenous Peoples: living and working conditions of aboriginal peoples in independent countries", which contained the first detailed study of this issue.

Convention No. 107

In 1957, the International Labour Conference adopted the first instrument specifically aimed at internationally recognising and guaranteeing various minimum rights for indigenous and tribal peoples: Convention No. 107 *"concerning the protection and integration of indigenous and other tribal and semi-tribal populations in independent countries"*.

Its 37 **articles** refer to the protection of the institutions, people, goods and work of indigenous peoples; the individual and collective ownership of traditional lands; the interdiction of forced removals; compensation in the case of loss or damage caused by removals; the protection of indigenous workers in relation to recruitment and labour conditions and the prohibition of discrimination; the right to vocational training, to social security and health care and to education in indigenous languages. This Convention also obliges States to adopt educational measures in order to eliminate prejudices amongst the rest of the national population which affect the image and rights of indigenous peoples.

> Convention No. 107 was ratified by 27 countries. At the end of 1998 it was still in effect in the following States: Angola, Argentina, Bangladesh, Belgium, Brazil, Cuba, Ecuador, Egypt, Ghana, Guinea-Bissau, Haiti, India, Iraq, Malawi, Panama, Pakistan, Portugal, Dominican Republic, El Salvador, Syrian Arab Republic and Tunisia.

Convention No. 107 was complemented by **Recommendation No. 104**, which proposes legislative or administrative measures to regulate the conditions of access of indigenous peoples to the land and its resources, as well as the establishment of a system of cooperative credit and modern production, supply and marketing methods adapted to collective forms of land ownership. The recommendation also suggests regulatory measures to govern the hiring of indigenous workers, in order to protect their salaries and personal freedom, to facilitate their adaptation to modern working conditions and their new socio-economic environment and to encourage their vocational training. Finally, it makes proposals regarding administration social security, health care, education, language and the media, and the protection of nomadic groups whose traditional territories extend across international borders.

Convention No. 169

During the 1970s, Convention No. 107 was harshly critised for its integrationalist spirit and because it assumed that decisions relating to the development of indigenous peoples were the responsibility of governments and not of the communities themselves. A large number of indigenous organizations questioned this focus and asked for it to be amended.

In 1988 and 1989 the International Labour Conference carried out a **partial revision of Convention No. 107** which brought about a **new convention**, no. 169, called the *"Convention concerning indigenous and tribal populations in independent countries"*, which was proclaimed in

1989. This Convention replaces no. 107 for those countries which decided to ratify it. The States Parties to Convention No. 107 which have still not ratified no. 169 remain obliged to comply with the measures of the former.

> **Convention No. 169** recognises the aspiration of indigenous peoples to control their own institutions, their way of life and economic development and to preserve and develop their identity, language and religion. It demands full recognition of and respect for the values, social, cultural, religious and spiritual practices and institutions of indigenous peoples. It introduces the **principle of consultation** with institutions which are representative of indigenous peoples and communities with regard to legislation and administrative measures of concern to them and encourages their **participation** in decision making at a local, regional and national level.

According to Convention No. 169, it is for indigenous peoples themselves to **decide their own priorities** regarding to development and to participate directly in national and regional plans and programmes affecting them. These must have as their main objective, the improvement of their living and working conditions and the raising of their levels of education and health care. It also recommends the implementation of **studies to evaluate the impact** - social, spiritual, cultural and environmental - of development plans on indigenous peoples, in cooperation with them, and demands measures for the **protection and preservation of the environment** within their territories.

Other important issues dealt with in this convention are:
- **recognition of customs and of customary indigenous law**, provided they are compatible with the national legal system and internationally recognised human rights;
- **labour rights**, including equality in the areas of vocational training, employment and remuneration, medical assistance and social security, the right of association, the protection of seasonal and migrant workers, the interdiction of debt servitude and the protection of indigenous women from sexual harassment;
- the provision of adequate **health services**;
- the recognition of the importance of **traditional economic activities**;
- the participation of indigenous peoples in the design and implementation of **educational** programmes and services, the right to create their own institutions and forms of education, to teach their children to read and write - if possible in both their own language

and the official language of the country in which they live - and to have available **mass media** in their own languages;
- **contacts and cooperation** between indigenous peoples across national borders;
- the establishment of national institutions to manage programmes relating to indigenous peoples, in close cooperation with them.

Some of the most important measures in Convention No. 169 refer to **territorial rights** (Articles 13 to 19). Considering the special importance of the relationship between indigenous peoples and the land, their right to property and possession of the lands which they traditionally occupy is recognised and the right of access to other lands where they habitually carry out traditional and subsistence activities is safeguarded. The Convention also establishes respect for the rights of indigenous peoples over the natural resources within their territories and demands that they should be consulted if prospecting or mineral exploitation activities are to be commenced on their lands. Indigenous peoples should share in the profits derived from these activities and should be compensated for any damage caused by them.

Only in exceptional cases does it allow for the **displacement** of indigenous peoples, provided that the **free and informed consent of the communities affected** has been obtained. As far as possible, they must be allowed to return to their lands once the motives that led to their displacement have come to an end. Otherwise they must be given lands of at least equal quality and legal status so that they may satisfy their material needs and ensure their future development or, if they prefer, receive appropriate compensation. Finally, the **methods of transmission of territorial rights** characteristic of indigenous peoples are recognised, and ways of avoiding and punishing invasions of their lands and dishonest manoeuvrings to strip them of their territorial rights are provided for. It establishes that national agrarian programmes must guarantee indigenous peoples conditions equivalent to those of the rest of the population with regard to the provision of land and the technical means for making it productive.

> As with any treaty which is binding upon States which ratify it, **Convention No. 169 does not encompass the maximum aspirations of indigenous peoples**, but it does formulate a series of **minimum** standards, respect for which on the part of governments would, in many cases, enable an improvement in their living and working conditions. Despite the fact that it constitutes a great step forward in relation to Convention No. 107, some indigenous organizations and peoples strongly criticise it and are opposed to its ratification on the part of the States in which they live.

Many indigenous people (above all in the United States and Canada) consider it to be very negative for various reasons. Firstly, in spite of talking of "peoples" (and not "populations", as previously), **it does not recognise the right of indigenous peoples to self-determination**. Secondly, the principle of recourse to consultation with their representative institutions is much more vague and easily manipulated by governments than the requirement for their **free and informed consent**. In effect, it creates no guarantees that it will be the indigenous peoples and communities themselves who decide on the representativeness of their institutions, thus leaving it open to possible manipulation on the part of governments. Consultation, furthermore, is not binding on the part of governments, whilst the need for free and informed consent in fact signifies a right of veto on the part of indigenous peoples with regard to decisions affecting them. Thirdly, **the interdiction of forced displacements of indigenous peoples from their lands is not absolute** and the exceptional circumstances which could justify removals of this kind are not listed. It is thus the governments which, decide if there is a need to displace them or not. Fourthly, indigenous peoples' control of resources within their territories is limited, because **it does not include subsoil resources** which, in the majority of countries, are considered the property of the State, nor other resources which States may appropriate, as is often the case with **water and forestry resources**.

In spite of these significant limitations, many indigenous peoples and organizations consider that Convention No.169 is a significant step forward with regard to recognition of their fundamental rights and they demand that their national governments ratify it.

> As of December 1998, Convention No.169 had been ratified by the following countries: Bolivia, Colombia, Costa Rica, Denmark, Ecuador, Fiji, Guatemala, Honduras, Mexico, Norway, Netherlands, Paraguay and Peru.

Other ILO conventions of relevance to indigenous peoples

There are other instruments of the International Labour Organization which may be invoked by indigenous peoples, provided the States in which they live have ratified them. They are Convention No. 50 on the recruitment of indigenous workers (1936); Convention No. 64 on contracts of employment for indigenous workers and Convention No. 65 on penal sanctions for indigenous workers (1939); Convention No. 86 on contracts of employment (1947); Convention No. 105 on the abolition of forced labour (1957); Convention No. 111 (1958) on the elimination of discrimination and the promotion of equal opportunities in employment, and Convention No. 141 (1975) on rural workers' organizations.

> For more information on the international standards drawn up by the ILO, you can call (41 22) 799-7126, fax (41 22) 799-6926 or send an email to the following address: infleg@ilo.org

- *The ILO's technical assistance programmes*

Apart from formulating and monitoring international legal standards, the ILO studies the labour situation and its tendencies at a global level, investigates employment generating activities, increases in productivity and social protection, promotes the negotiation of labour agreements between parties at a national level, and develops programmes of technical assistance and advice in countries of the Third World. These programmes lay the foundations for the said countries to subsequently ratify the ILO conventions.

Various **technical cooperation programmes** promote the training of indigenous peoples themselves in the formulation and implementation of their projects, in diverse areas of work:
- the recovery of ecologically degraded lands in order to reforest them and relaunch commercial agriculture, as a means to improve the living conditions of the indigenous population;
- the demarcation of traditional territories and the legalisation of land tenure;
- the development of cooperatives in order to create employment and income opportunities amongst indigenous people dispossessed of their traditional means of subsistence;
- vocational training and financial assistance to indigenous women in situations of extreme poverty;
- small-scale public works to establish or improve basic infrastructure in rural areas (roads, irrigation channels, reforestation etc.) and to solve the problem of unemployment amongst the indigenous work force in these regions;
- the recovery of traditional craft techniques and training in marketing techniques in order to improve domestic incomes and strengthen the worth of their culture;
- the strengthening of indigenous organizations and their capacity to formulate development projects in accordance with their own priorities and work methods.

These technical assistance programmes are open to all indigenous organizations, which should present their proposals directly to the ILO.

> Development Policies Branch,
> International Labour Office,
> 4, route des Morillons,
> 1211 Geneva 22 - SWITZERLAND
> Tel: (41 22) 799-6931 Fax: (41 22) 798-8685
> Email: webinfo@ilo.org   Website: http://www.ilo.org

2. The United Nations Educational, Scientific and Cultural Organization (UNESCO)

- *Its objectives and structure*

UNESCO was founded in 1946 to promote peaceful collaboration between nations through education, science and culture. Amongst the fundamental objectives of UNESCO are: the reduction of illiteracy, the dissemination of scientific know-how, the facilitation of scientific, educational and cultural communication and exchanges at a world level and the preservation of humanity's artistic and cultural heritage.

In order to achieve these goals, UNESCO organizes its activities around five main functions: promoting studies on the role of education, science and culture in the world of tomorrow; developing, transferring and sharing knowledge; formulating international standards; providing technical assistance to governments and exchanging specialist information.

UNESCO is made up of:
- the **General Conference**, in which all the Member States are represented[2]. It deals with the formulation of policies and approval of the organization's programmes and budget.
- the **Executive Board**, whose 58 members are elected by the General Conference. It meets two or three times per year to supervise programme implementation.
- the **Secretariat**, headed by the Director-General, which deals with programme implementation.

UNESCO's headquarters are in Paris, France. UNESCO also **has national commissions**, in which the relevant government departments and non-governmental organizations are represented. These deal with issues relating to education, science and culture.

- *UNESCO and human rights*

UNESCO promotes human rights largely through **education and dissemination activities** such as studies, courses, seminars and informational material.

It also drafts **international instruments** for the promotion and protection of various fundamental human rights such as the right to education, to information, to international cultural cooperation and to the protection of interests resulting from any literary or artistic production. It furthermore defends the right to participate in cultural life and in scientific progress, as well as the right to a cultural identity and to the protection of intellectual property and cultural heritage.

- *Supervision of UNESCO conventions*

The principal monitoring mechanism of these instruments is the **presentation of periodic reports** on the part of States Parties regarding the measures adopted at a national level to put into practice the obligations contracted on ratifying a UNESCO Convention. These reports are studied by the **Committee on Conventions and Recommendations** on Education, a body composed of representatives of the Member States of UNESCO which meets twice a year and which does not accept supplementary information provided by non-governmental organizations or individuals. **Only in the case of the Convention against Discrimination in Education is there a mechanism for the submission of complaints** which may be used by one State Party against another but not by individuals, for which reason it is very little used.

Nevertheless, in 1978 UNESCO adopted a procedure for the **submission of individual complaints regarding individual or mass violations of rights** which affect issues within its competence (education, science, culture or communication), even though they may be being dealt with or already been dealt with by other international bodies. These include cases of detention, torture and mistreatment, executions, forced exile, denial of legal status, censure, freedom of conscience, expression or thought and religion, intellectual property rights and the cultural rights of minorities, amongst others.

> This procedure, established in **decision 104 Ex/Decision 3.3**, may be used against any Member State of UNESCO, having ratified this organization's conventions or not. Either the direct victim or his or her family, an NGO or any other person or group with direct credible and well-founded information on events may commence this process.

This procedure **is confidential** as neither the steps taken, nor UNESCO's conclusions and recommendations, are made publicly known, but the identity of the plaintiff and the victim are always revealed to the government in question. Complaints can thus never be anonymous. They must not be formulated in an insulting manner, nor be based on exclusively political motives or on solely journalistic information. They must be submitted within a "reasonable length of time" after events have occurred, indicating which domestic recourses have been used to resolve the situation. They must also be written in one of the two working languages of UNESCO: English or French.

- *What UNESCO does with the complaints it receives*

When a written complaint arrives at the UNESCO Secretariat, the **Office of International Standards and Legal Affairs** acknowledges receipt and informs the plaintiff of the conditions of admissibility. At this time it sends him or her a form to fill in, on which all information about the case must be included. Only when UNESCO receives the duly completed form will it begin to process the complaint.

This is then transmitted to the State in question, providing it with a certain length of time within which to submit its comments. When the government's response is received, or when the period of time expires, the Office of International Standards and Legal Affairs passes the complaint on to the **Committee on Conventions and Recommendations** in order that it may study its admissibility. Representatives of the government may participate in these sessions in order to provide additional information or respond to questions. The **Director-General of UNESCO** then communicates the Committee's decision to the plaintiff and to the government regarding the **admissibility of the complaint.** Generally, most cases are deferred until the following session of the Committee so that a humanitarian solution may be sought for them.

Communications considered admissible then move onto an in-depth examination by the Committee in order to decide whether "they merit being processed or not", or whether they must continue to be studied whilst a friendly solution is sought or whether the Executive Board must be recommended to take decisive measures. In any case, **both the plaintiff and the government are informed of the Committee's decision**. The Committee then submits a confidential report with its recommendations to the Executive Board, which analyses it in a private session.

In urgent cases of human rights violations, UNESCO's Director-General carries out **humanitarian action** through confidential consultations with the parties.

- *UNESCO instruments of interest to indigenous peoples*
- The 1960 **Convention against Discrimination in Education** has as its objective the elimination of all discrimination within the field of education which may be motivated by race, colour, sex, language, religion, political opinion, national or social origin, financial state or birth and to promote equality of opportunities for all with regard to education. It contains measures to eliminate discriminatory legislative

and administrative measures and to bring about compulsory and free primary education as well as free access to secondary education and to higher education. Article 5 recognises the right of national minorities to have access to their own educational activities, including management of schools and the use and teaching of their own language.

- **The Declaration on the principles of international cultural cooperation** of 1966 considers that ignorance regarding the way of life and traditions of different peoples represents an obstacle to friendship and peaceful cooperation between nations. It affirms that each culture has dignity and value which must be respected and preserved and that each people has the right and the duty to develop its culture. The variety and diversity of all cultures is a common heritage of humanity.
- **The Recommendation concerning Education for international understanding, cooperation and peace and Education relating to human rights and fundamental freedoms** of 1974 affirms that the Member States of UNESCO must promote the study of different cultures, perspectives and ways of life, their reciprocal influences all levels in the education system so that differences may be mutually appreciated.
- In 1978 UNESCO proclaimed the **Declaration on race and racial prejudice** which affirms that all peoples and human groups contribute in their own way to the progress of cultures and civilisation and that they constitute the common heritage of humanity. Both individuals and groups have the right to be different and to consider themselves and be perceived by others as different, without the diversity of ways of life serving as a pretext for racial prejudice and without legitimising any type of discriminatory practice. All human beings thus have the right to maintain their cultural identity and to freely develop their intellectual, technical, social, economic, cultural and political identity. Each group may freely decide whether it wishes to maintain, adapt or enrich the values it considers essential to its identity and States have a responsibility to ensure that educational resources (school programmes and books, teacher training courses, means of communication) are devoted to combating racism and to promoting understanding, tolerance and friendship between human groups. National law must forbid all racist propaganda, organizations or practices. The Declaration on Race and Racial Prejudice also affirms the need to give special attention to marginalized racial or ethnic groups in order to assure them the protection of the law and social benefits in the areas of housing, employment and health, respecting their culture and values and facilitating their social and professional promotion.
- UNESCO has drawn up a draft **Universal Declaration on the Human Genome and Human Rights** which affirms that the human

genome emphasizes the importance of the fundamental unity of all members of the human family and thus constitutes, in a symbolic sense, a common heritage of humanity. Every human being has the right to expect his or her dignity and rights to be respected, regardless of his or her genetic characteristics, to which nobody can be reduced. The unique character and diversity of human beings must also be respected.
- In 1993, the Seminar on Education, Labour and Cultural Pluralism organized by UNESCO and UNESCO's Mexican Commission approved the **Declaration of Oaxaca**, which states that the development of cultural pluralism will only be possible once respect for the equal dignity of all cultures has been introduced in Latin America and once dialogue and cooperation have become alternatives to intolerance, exclusion and violence. The Declaration of Oaxaca proclaims respect for indigenous cultures and for their special relationship with nature. Participants in this Seminar agreed to promote constitutional and legislative developments in order to encourage the rights of indigenous peoples, to establish commissions in this respect and to create legal offices responsible for monitoring the human rights of indigenous peoples, amongst other things.

- *Other UNESCO activities of relevance to indigenous peoples*

For many years UNESCO has developed **programmes focussed around literacy** for indigenous peoples and around access to education, encouraging bilingualism and pluriculturalism. On the occasion of the 500th anniversary of Columbus' arrival in the Americas and during the International Year of the World's Indigenous Peoples (1993), UNESCO **supported a number of meetings** which enabled different indigenous peoples from the Americas to come together and also to meet government representatives and noteworthy intellectuals in order to initiate a constructive dialogue and to raise awareness amongst the rest of society regarding their living conditions and their aspirations.

UNESCO also provides **technical support to indigenous peoples** through projects aimed at increasing their capacity for management of their own development and at preserving their languages and traditional handicrafts.

More information can be obtained by writing to:

UNESCO,
7, place de Fontenoy,
75352 Paris 07 SP, France.
Tel: (33 1) 45-681000 / Fax: (33 1) 45-671690
Web page: http://www.unesco.org
Telex: 204461, Paris - 270602, Paris

3. The Food and Agriculture Organization (FAO)

- *Its objectives and structure*

The FAO was established in 1945 in order to improve the nutritional status and improve the living conditions of the world's population through an increase in agricultural productivity. It works out statistics regarding nutritional levels, agricultural production and the state of forestry and fishery resources and studies how agricultural goods are produced, distributed and consumed. It promotes national and international action to improve the production and marketing of these goods in order to ensure the conservation of natural resources and to develop agricultural credit policies. It also provides technical assistance around these and other issues such as nutrition, agricultural engineering, agrarian reform, communications, technology transfer and the prevention of food losses. It also publishes informational material.

The FAO is made up of a **Conference of Member States** which meets every two years to decide organizational policy, a **Council** composed of 49 Member States appointed by the Conference for a period of three years and a **Secretariat** made up of professionals and headed by a Director-General, with a six year mandate. The FAO organizes its work into eight departments: Administration and Finance, General Affairs and Information, Social and Economic Policy, Technical Cooperation, Agriculture, Fisheries, Forestry and Sustainable Development.

As of December, 1998, the FAO had 175 Member States. Its headquarters are in Rome, but it has regional offices in all five continents.

- *FAO activities of interest to indigenous peoples*

The FAO **has not formulated any international legal instruments**, but it carries out **agricultural promotion activities** and **food programmes for vulnerable groups** in the field. Some of them involve indigenous peoples directly: the Plan of Action for Peoples' Participation in Rural Development, the Freedom from Hunger Programme and the Forests, Trees and People Programme. In Peru, it works with the indigenous peoples of the Altiplano (high plateau) in order to increase food production and use reforestation to generate energy and rural development. The FAO also participates in activities which **implement Agenda 21 and the Convention on Biodiversity** with regard to the conservation and use of genetic resources and the transmission of indigenous peoples' traditional knowledge on resource management. Together with the United Nations, the FAO sponsors the **World Food Programme**.

For more information, write to:

> Food and Agriculture Organization (FAO)
> Vialle delle Terme di Caracalla
> 00100 Rome,
> ITALY
> Tel: (39 6) 57-051 / Fax: (39 6) 570-53152
> Telex: 625852 / 625853 / 610181 FAO I
> Email: postmaster@fao.org
> Web site: http://www.fao.org

4. The World Health Organization (WHO)

- *Its objectives and structure*

The WHO, established in 1948, is the coordinating body for work carried out internationally in the field of health. It attempts to design projects to eradicate endemic illnesses and epidemics and concentrates its greatest efforts in the area of primary health care, that is, in the **prevention of illnesses**.

In order to do this, the WHO promotes the improvement of the health and sanitation conditions of the population through health education, the installation of drinking water and sewage systems, the diversification and strengthening of nutritional intake, vaccination campaigns, mother and child care and the provision of essential medicines. In cooperation with other specialized agencies, the WHO also carries out research and training programmes around different types of illnesses. Another of the organization's activities is improving the levels of education and training of health care professionals, the establishment of international standards for biological and pharmaceutical products and the harmonizing of diagnostic methods. It also provides technical assistance to governments who require it in order to improve their health services. It publishes a great deal of informational material.

The WHO is controlled by the **World Health Assembly**, in which are represented all of the Member States (191 as of December 1998). It meets once a year to decide the policy, programme and budget of the organization. An **Executive Board** of 31 members, elected by the World Assembly, meets twice a year to carry out the decisions of the Assembly. The **Secretariat** is headed by a Director-General and is composed of technical and administrative staff. The WHO's headquarters is in Geneva, but there are regional organizations which coordinate a large part of the work in each region.

- *WHO activities of interest to indigenous peoples*

The WHO has actively participated in the standard-setting activities of the UN and the ILO, providing helpful suggestions for the inclusion of articles relating to health in ILO Convention Nos. 107 and 169 and in the draft United Nations Declaration on the Rights of Indigenous Peoples.

Although the WHO **has no special department to deal with the health of indigenous peoples**, the 47th session of the World Health Assembly, which met in 1994, decided that the organization should be involved in the planning and implementation of the International Decade of the World's Indigenous Peoples and asked its regional offices to set up **groups of indigenous advisors** with special knowledge of the needs and health resources of their communities. During the International Decade, the WHO will attempt to promote respect for, and preservation of, the knowledge, remedies and medical traditions of indigenous peoples and will join in health projects of concern to indigenous peoples and communities.

For more information write to:

> World Health Organization (WHO)
> 20, Avenue Appia
> 1211, Geneva 27
> SWITZERLAND
> Tel: (41 22) 791-2111 / Fax: (41 22) 791-0746
> Email: info@who.ch
> Web site: http://www.who.org

5. The World Bank

- *Its structure and objectives*

The World Bank is made up of three different financial institutions created between 1945 and 1960: the **International Bank for Reconstruction and Development (IBRD)**, established in 1945 to facilitate the reconstruction and development of Member States; the **International Finance Corporation**, set up in 1956 to finance private companies which invest in development activities and the **International Development Association**, founded in 1960 to provide loans to poor countries.

The World Bank provides **loans** for productive activities and **technical assistance** to Member States, government agencies and private businesses which have the backing of a State guarantee. In theory, its objective is to raise standards of living in less developed countries with financial resources generated by the developed world and invested in projects directed at health, education, environmental protection, support to the private sector and improvement in State services, amongst other things. The World Bank also publishes **studies and statistical information** on issues such as agriculture and rural development, economic and social conditions, education, financing and debt, demography and public health, business, transport and urban development.

- *The World Bank and indigenous peoples*

With the supposed aim of contributing to the "development" of poor countries, the World Bank has financed many large undertakings which have had harmful consequences on the lives of indigenous peoples: hydroelectric dams which transformed the habitat of a large number of groups, forcing them to move and often to migrate to the cities in search of alternative sources of work; roads and routes which facilitated the invasion and exploitation of indigenous territories by multinational companies, landless settlers and gold prospectors, amongst other things.

From the 1980s onwards, a new sensitivity has been noted in the World Bank towards the economic, social and cultural consequences of its projects on the indigenous peoples affected. Officially, it decided not to support development projects which knowingly involve the usurpation of the traditional territories of tribal peoples, unless adequate alternatives were provided. In the 1990s, the World Bank emphasised the need to promote the informed participation of indigenous peoples in projects which concerned them and affirmed that the social and economic benefits of the development process should be shared.

Currently, various World Bank projects include **Indigenous Development Plans** which promote training in the formulation of small-scale projects and in the techniques of accountancy, the establishment of cooperatives and of small rural industry, the management of natural resources and the conservation of forestry resources. The World Bank is also developing studies on poverty and indigenous peoples in Latin America and an analysis of the health and nutritional situation of the tribal peoples of India.

- *The World Bank Small Grants Programme*

The World Bank has a programme of small grants aimed at **supporting modest projects of environmental management and preservation of traditional knowledge** in the areas of the environment, nutrition, health, agro-industrial development etc.

Any non-profit making, non-governmental organization may request a grant of this type from the World Bank. In general, the Bank only finances 50% of the cost of projects submitted to it. It is necessary to write to the World Bank with information regarding:

- the organization requesting the grant (its objectives, staff, current activities and sources of funding);
- the activities for which the grant is requested (description of the project, of the estimated budget and how you expect to spend the money, the time considered necessary to carry out the project and, possibly, a list of those participating in the activities described);
- other donors from whom money has been requested or who have already agreed to provide funds for the project;
- how previous grants provided by the World Bank were used.

For more information write to:

> Small Grants Programme,
> World Bank,
> 1818 H. Street, N.W.
> Washington, D.C. 20433
> UNITED STATES OF AMERICA
> Tel: (1 202) 473-1767 / Fax: (1 202) 676-0574 or 477-6391
> Web site: http://www.worldbank.org

6. The United Nations Development Programme (UNDP)

- *Its objectives and main activities*

The United Nations Development Programme (UNDP) commenced operations in 1965 on the basis of annual voluntary contributions from the Member States of the UN devoted to finance **technical assistance programmes** for those governments which requested them. Its objective is to help **underdeveloped countries** to put their human and natural resources to better use in order to increase standards of living and economic productivity. Approximately 80% of the UNDP's country programme funds are aimed at countries which have an annual per capita income of $750 or less.

The UNDP has its headquarters in New York and is supervised by an **Executive Board** of 36 members, representatives of the developed and underdeveloped world. It carries out activities in more than 170 countries and has offices in 134 countries, headed by a **resident representative**. In close cooperation with the other United Nations agencies, which provide specialised technical assistance, the UNDP coordinates development projects in different areas: agricultural production, fishing, forestry, mining, manufacturing, generation of electricity, communications and transport, health and nutrition, environmental protection, education and training, economic planning, public administration reform and community development.

- *The UNDP and indigenous peoples*

Amongst the projects supported by United Nations Development Programme are some which benefit indigenous communities directly, having as their main objective the assurance of adequate levels of health, nutrition and social security and the protection of the human rights, territories, natural resources, cultures and intellectual property rights of indigenous peoples.

> Through resources aimed at **country programmes**, the UNDP supports small-scale projects aimed at eradicating poverty, improving living conditions, encouraging community participation, conserving the environment and natural resources and revitalising traditional cultures.

Projects of this type should be submitted to the national development agency or to the UNDP office in-country and should be no greater than $50,000. The support they receive will depend on national development priorities as defined by the respective government.

For more information, write to the UNDP office in your country or to:

> United Nations Development Programme,
> 1, United Nations Plaza,
> New York, NY 10017
> UNITED STATES OF AMERICA
> Tel: (1 212) 906-5000 / Fax: (1 212) 906-5313
> Web site: http://www.undp.org

7. The International Fund for Agricultural Development (IFAD)

- *Its objectives, structure and activities*

The International Fund for Agricultural Development was established at the end of 1977 in order to mobilize resources aimed at **improving the food production and nutrition** of the most marginalized rural groups and of those with the lowest incomes in the underdeveloped countries. Its activities thus focus on the **most vulnerable groups in rural societies**: smallholders, landless peasants, pastoral nomads, fisherpeople, poor women, refugees and displaced persons.

IFAD provides **loans at a very low rate of interest** for projects aimed at generating employment and improving agricultural production, nutritional levels and the distribution of income amongst these social sectors. The projects are increasingly defined, implemented and evaluated with the close participation of the beneficiary groups themselves.

Apart from credit, IFAD provides **technical assistance** in the area of agriculture, as well as **legal assistance and training** in literacy programmes.

This Fund is supervised by a **Governing Council** which includes all the Member States of this agency (161 at the end of 1998), divided into three categories: developed countries, developing countries which contribute to the Fund and beneficiary countries. There is also an **Executive Board** of 18 members which supervises the operations carried out and which is headed by the **President** of the Fund.

- *IFAD and indigenous peoples*

In recent years, IFAD has begun to take an interest in the situation of indigenous peoples and supports projects aimed at creating the appropriate conditions for the preservation of their ways of life and the strengthening of their cultures. In Latin America IFAD supports projects for the demarcation of indigenous territories, the strengthening of indigenous organizations, the recuperation and dissemination of traditional technologies in agriculture, handicrafts and the management of forestry resources, strengthening of cultural identity through bilingual and multicultural education and the promotion of traditional medicines, amongst other things.

For more information write to:

> International Fund for Agricultural Development,
> Vía del Seráfico 107
> 00142 Rome
> ITALY
> Tel: (39 6) 54-591 / Fax: (39 6) 504-3463
> Web site: http://www.unicc.org/ifad/home.html

8) World Intellectual Property Organization (WIPO)

- *Its objectives*

The World Intellectual Property Organization was established in 1967 with the mandate of stimulating human creativity to promote the protection of intellectual property throughout the world. The two main branches of intellectual property are **industrial property** (chiefly inventions, trademarks, industrial designs and models and appellations of origin); and **copyright** (chiefly literary, musical, artistic, photographic and audiovisual works). To achieve its objectives, the WIPO carries out cooperation activities with governments and administers a series of treaties on the different technical aspects of intellectual property. At the beginning of 1997, WIPO had 161 Member States.

- *WIPO and indigenous peoples*

WIPO's interest in issues of intellectual property which affect the traditional knowledge of indigenous peoples is very recent. In March 1998, a **Global Intellectual Property Issues Division** was created within the organization, with the aim of exploring and investigating the needs and expectations of the new potential beneficiaries of intellectual property, the most important being indigenous peoples. In July of this year this new division held a Round Table on Intellectual Property and Indigenous Peoples at its headquarters in Geneva in which, for the first time, some two hundred indigenous representatives were able to dialogue with civil servants and representatives of the Member States of WIPO in order to gain information on existing mechanisms for the protection of intellectual property and to exchange experiences amongst themselves on the issue of the protection of their traditional knowledge. Other activities of the recently created Global Intellectual Property Issues Division are survey missions in the field in various places around the world inhabited by indigenous people and pilot projects for documenting how traditional knowledge is formed, as well as how to apply information technology progress to the protection and conservation of the said knowledge.

For more information, contact:

```
Global Intellectual Property Issues Division
World Intellectual Property Organization
34, rue des Colombettes
1211 Geneva 20
SWITZERLAND
Tel: (41 22) 338-9319
Fax: (41 22) 338-8120
Email: richard.owens@wipo.int
General email for WIPO: wipo.mail@wipo.int
Web site: http://www.wipo.int
        http://www.ompi.int
```

8. Other UNO agencies of interest to indigenous peoples

- The United Nations High Commissioner for Refugees (UNHCR)
  William Rappard Centre,
  154, rue de Lausanne
  1202, Geneva
  SWITZERLAND
  Tel: (41 22) 739-8111 / Fax: (41 22) 731-9546
  Web site: http://www.unchr.ch

- The United Nations Children's Fund (UNICEF)
  Pavillons du Petit-Saconnex
  16, avenue Jean Trembley
  1209, Geneva
  SWITZERLAND
  Tel: (41 22) 798-5850 / Fax: (41 22) 791-0822
  Web site: http://www.unicef.org

- The United Nations Industrial Development Organization (UNIDO)
  Vienna International Centre,
  PO Box 300,
  A - 1400, Vienna
  AUSTRIA
  Tel: (43 1) 21-130 / Fax: (43 1) 23-2126
  Web site: http://www.unido.org

Notes

[1] As of December 1998 the ILO had 174 Member States.
[2] As of December 1998, UNESCO had 186 Member States.

CHAPTER 5

BIBLIOGRAPHIC JOURNEY

1. Fact Sheets of the UN Centre for Human Rights

Of the documents consulted in the course of this work, we would highlight the *Fact Sheets on Human Rights* published by the Centre for Human Rights in Geneva. The aim of the *Fact Sheets* is to provide information on fundamental human rights, the UN activities in promoting and protecting them and the international mechanisms in existence to ensure their effective respect.

Freely distributed throughout the world, the *Fact Sheets* may be reproduced in other languages provided that their content is not changed in any way and that the source of information is cited. When requesting copies, you must state the language, number of copies and full title required.

The Fact Sheets are available on the Internet: http//www.unhchr.ch

Fact Sheets published by the Centre for Human Rights:

N° 1   *Human Rights Machinery*
N° 2   *The International Bill of Human Rights*
N° 3   *Advisory Services and Technical Cooperation in the field of Human Rights*
N° 4   *Methods of Combating Torture*
N° 5   *Programme of Action for the Second Decade to Combat Racism and Racial Discrimination*
N° 6   *Enforced or Involuntary Disappearances*
N° 7   *Communications Procedures*
N° 8   *World Public Information Campaign for Human Rights*
N° 9   *The Rights of Indigenous Peoples*
N° 10 *The Rights of the Child*
N° 11 *Extrajudicial, Summary or Arbitrary Executions*
N° 12 *The Committee on the Elimination of Racial Discrimination*
N° 13 *International Humanitarian Law and Human Rights*
N° 14 *Contemporary Forms of Slavery*
N° 15 *Civil and Political Rights: the Human Rights Committee*
N° 16 *The Committee on Economic, Social and Cultural Rights*
N° 17 *The Committee Against Torture*
N° 18 *Minority Rights*

N° 19 *National Institutions for the Promotion and Protection of Human Rights*
N° 20 *Human Rights and Refugees*
N° 21 *The Human Right to Adequate Housing*
N° 22 *Discrimination against Women: the Convention and the Committee*
N° 23 *Harmful Traditional Practices Affecting the Health of Women and Children*
N° 24 *The Rights of Migrant Workers*
N° 25 *Forced Evictions and Human Rights*

2. Human Rights Study Series

These works consist of studies and reports drawn up by experts from the Commission on Human Rights and the Sub-Commission on different human rights issues:

N° 1 *The Right to Adequate Food as a Human Right*
N° 2 *The Elimination of All Forms of Intolerance and Discrimination based on Religion or Belief*
N° 3 *Study on the Freedom of the Individual under Law: an analysis of Article 29 of the Universal Declaration*
N° 4 *Status of the Individual and Contemporary International Law: Promotion, Protection and Restoration of Human Rights at National, Regional and International Levels*
N° 5 *Study on the Rights of Persons Belonging to Ethnic, Religious and Linguistic Minorities*
N° 6 *Human Rights and Disabled Persons*
N° 7 *The Right to Adequate Housing*
N° 8 *Sexual Exploitation of Children*

3. Official Documents of the United Nations

These documents have a **document symbol** which identifies them and indicates the organ which drew them up and what sort of document it is. They are usually published in English, French and Spanish. These codes are composed of letters and numbers and they identify the documents as official publications of the United Nations. Some are available on **general distribution** (which means they may be requested at any time), whilst others are available on **restricted distribution** (they may circulate only during the session at which the issue is to be discussed and amongst the participants) or **limited** distribution (these are generally drafts of texts which will later appear in a final version).

The following are some of the more frequently used abbreviations:

A/	General Assembly
E/	Economic and Social Council
S/	Security Council
ST/	Secretariat
CAT/C	Committee Against Torture
CCPR/C	Committee on Civil and Political Rights
CERD/C	Committee on the Elimination of Racial Discrimination
CESCR/C	Committee on Economic, Social and Cultural Rights
CEDAW/C	Committee for the Elimination of Discrimination Against Women
CRC/C	Committee on the Rights of the Child
HR/	Human Rights
DPI/	UN Department of Public Information

For the subsidiary organs, the "parent" organization from which the mandate came is always indicated first and then, following the bar, the type of organ that it is. Frequently used symbols are the following:

/C...	Committee
/CN...	Commission
/CONF...	Conference
/PC...	Preparatory Committee
/WG...	Working Group
/AC...	Ad hoc Committee, sometimes also called Working Groups.
/TM...	Technical Meeting

So the codes which appear further on must be read as follows:

E/CN.4/	Document of the Commission on Human Rights, a commission of the Economic and Social Council.
E/CN.4/Sub.2/	Document of the Sub-Commission on Prevention of Discrimination and Protection of Minorities, a subsidiary organ of the Commission on Human Rights.
E/CN.4/Sub.2/AC.4/	Document of the Working Group on Indigenous Populations, a working group of the Sub-Commission on Prevention of Discrimination and Protection of Minorities
E/CN.6/	Document of the Commission on the Status of Women

Following identification of the organ for which the document has been prepared appears a figure in arabic numerals which indicates either the session (A/47/...) or the corresponding year (E/CN.4/Sub.2/1995...). Sometimes this date is followed by a serial number, again in arabic numerals, which specifically identifies the document. Some of the codes which may appear after these identifiers are the following:

/Add.	Addendum (supplement)
/Corr.	Corrigendum (correction)
/Rev.	Revision (of a previously published text)
/L.	Document in limited distribution (generally draft resolutions or reports, which may only be obtained at the time of publication)
/R.	Document in restricted circulation (not generally available to NGOs or individuals)
/CRP	Conference room paper
/NGO	Document containing communications from Non-Governmental Organizations
/PR	Press Release

Not all of the United Nations documents are free. Some studies, reports, compilations of documents and works of a general nature are sold to the public by the Document Departments, both in Geneva and New York. In these cases, the documents also have a **sales code** which begins with a letter indicating the language of publication (S for Spanish, F for French and E for English), followed by a number made up of two figures which denotes the year of publication (89 for 1989, 90 for 1990 and so on), a figure in roman numerals which indicates the type of publication (according to the subject matter) and a final figure which indicates the order of appearance of the publication in the series which has been published in the same year in that same category (1 for the first, 2 for the second etc.).

The addresses of the Document Departments are:

in Geneva:	*in New York:*
Vente des Publications	Document Department
United Nations Office at Geneva	United Nations Headquarters
1211, Geneva 10	New York, N.Y. 10017
SWITZERLAND	UNITED STATES OF AMERICA

Important: Due to current budgetary restrictions, the UN has limited enormously the number of copies it publishes and the postal distribution of its documents. On the other hand, it has made them available to the public on the Internet, and distributes them in printed version during the meetings of the organs which are due to deal with the issue. A full list of the reports of the different UN organs may be consulted at the following website: http//www.un.org/Depts/dhl/unique. The complete texts of the most recent reports are available on the website of the High Commissioner for Human Rights: http//www.unhchr.ch. For NGOs which are unable to access the Internet, it is recommended that they request the Office of the High Commissioner to send them free the publications which are of interest to them, in case printed copies are available. In order to do this, information regarding your organization must be sent with the request, including your aims, the type of work you carry out, your postal address and, if possible, proof that you are unable to pay for the publications. The Office of the High Commissioner gives priority to organizations from the Third World. Write to:

> Office of the High Commissioner for Human Rights
> United Nations Office at Geneva
> 1211, Geneva 10
> Switzerland
> Tel: (41 22) 917-9159

a) Documents relating to Indigenous Peoples

1) *Annual report of the WGIP:*
   Report of the Working Group on Indigenous Populations on its (last) session: (example of 1998)E/CN.4/Sub.2/1998/16.
2) *Reports of the Working Group established by the Commission on Human Rights (Resolution 1995/32) to formulate a draft declaration (to 1998 inclusive):*
   E/CN.4/1996/84
   E/CN.4/1997/102
   E/CN.4/1998/106
3) *Studies and special reports published in previous years (some documents have only been published in English):*

- *Study of the Problem of Discrimination Against Indigenous Populations (known as the Martínez Cobo report): E/CN.4/Sub.2/1986/Add. 1-4.*
- *The Effects of Racism and Racial Discrimination on the Social and Economic Relations Between Indigenous Peoples and States (report of a seminar, Geneva, 16-20 January 1989): HR/PUB/89/5.*

- *Report of the Meeting of Experts to review the experience of countries in the operation of schemes of internal self-government for indigenous peoples (Nuuk, Greenland, 1991): E/CN.4/1992/42/Add.1*
- *Report of the United Nations Technical Conference on Practical Experience in the Realization of Sustainable and Environmentally Sound Self-Development of Indigenous Peoples. Santiago de Chile, May 1992: E/CN.4/Sub.2/1992/31*
- *Transnational Investments and Operations on the Lands of Indigenous Peoples. Reports of the United Nations Centre on Transnational Corporations: E/CN.4/Sub.2/AC.4/1991/Misc. 1;*
  E/CN.4/Sub.2/1992/54
  E/CN.4/Sub.2/1994/40
- Different reports and studies on intellectual property and the heritage of indigenous peoples:
  1) *Intellectual Property of Indigenous Peoples: concise report of the Secretary-General: E/CN.4/Sub.2/1992/30.*
  2) *Study on the Protection of the Cultural and Intellectual Property of Indigenous Peoples by the Sub-Commission's Special Rapporteur, Mrs. Erica-Irene Daes: E/CN.4/Sub.2/1993/28*
- *Protection of the heritage of indigenous peoples. Reports presented by the Special Rapporteur, Mrs. Erica-Irene Daes: E/CN.4/Sub.2/1994/31*
  E/CN.4/Sub.2/1995/26
  E/CN.4/Sub.2/1996/22

  4) *Study on Treaties, Agreements and other Constructive Arrangements between States and Indigenous Populations. Reports presented by the Special Rapporteur, Mr. Miguel Alfonso Martínez:* E/CN.4/Sub.2/1991/33
  E/CN.4/Sub.2/1992/32
  E/CN.4/Sub.2/1995/27
  E/CN.4/Sub.2/1996/23

The most recent publications are available on the Internet.

During meetings of the Working Group on Indigenous Populations (in the Palais des Nations), a large amount of material is made available to participants which has been prepared by the Office of the High Commissioner for Human Rights (information provided by governments, specialized agencies and non-governmental organizations regarding each point of the provisional agenda of the Working Group). This must be requested at the Documentation counter, next to door 40, preferably during the first day of the session.

b) Other official documents of the United Nations relating to the promotion and protection of human rights:

ABC, Teaching Human Rights. Practical Activities for Primary and Secondary Schools: GE.91-19139-January 1992-5000. Booklet designed for primary and secondary school teachers who wish to encourage an awareness and knowledge of human rights issues.

United Nations Action in the field of Human Rights: ST/HR/2/Rev.4, Sales N° S.94.XIV.11. Contains a description of the organs, specialized agencies and other United Nations agencies which deal with human rights, explanations of existing instruments for the protection of a broad range of rights, as well as information on the process international Human Rights standard-setting and monitoring activities.

Calendar of United Nations Conferences and Meetings. Published by the Conference Services Division and the Division of Interpreting and Meetings from February onwards each year, updated every month, it can be requested from the Documents Department of the United Nations in New York. In Geneva, it can be obtained from the Documentation section, building B, door 40, 1st floor. It provides information on the dates and places of all meetings anticipated for that year. This information is currently available on the Internet, at the website of the High Commissioner for Human Rights.

Human Rights, Questions and Answers: DPI/919. A short leaflet aimed at a non-specialized audience, which contains a series of questions and answers designed to explain what basic human rights are, what the United Nations does to protect and promote them and what the existing mechanisms of application of these rights are.

Integrating human rights with sustainable human development: UNDP, 1998. A working document produced by the United Nations Development Programme about the relationship between human rights and sustainable human development. It describes the main activities of the UNDP in support of human rights and reflects on the integration of a human rights dimension into the work of this agency, both internally in the tasks it carries out in particular countries and in its relations with the United Nations Office of the High Commissioner for Human Rights. It is available on the Internet.

Teaching about Decolonisation: DPI/751 and DPI/751 Add.1, November 1984. A brief guide explaining the role of the United Nations in the process of decolonisation and proposing general suggestions for the teaching of the subject in schools.

List of Non-Governmental Organizations in consultative status with ECOSOC: 1992/NGO list parts 1/11. It includes up to date addresses, telephone and fax numbers for these NGOs. In English/French only.

Human Rights and Socio-Economic Development: a Selection of Publications: DPI/1028. A list of informative publications on human rights and development (in French and English).

Manual on Human Rights Reporting: HR/PUB/91/1, Sales N° S.91.XIV.1. Aimed at government officials responsible for preparing the periodic reports to UN Human Rights Treaty bodies. It is also very useful for NGOs wishing to participate in the work of these bodies and in the study of government reports. It contains suggestions for the presentation of reports under six international instruments and a good bibliography.

Second Decade to Combat Racism and Racial Discrimination: Global compilation of national legislation against racial discrimination: HR/PUB/90/8. A compilation drawn up on the basis of government responses to a questionnaire prepared by the Centre for Human Rights.

A compilation of international instruments: ST/HR/1/Rev.5, Sales N°: S.94.XIV.1. Contains the full texts of the international instruments of a universal nature - Declarations, Covenants, Conventions, Resolutions and Protocols - proclaimed by the United Nations system up to 31st March 1993.

Status of International Instruments: ST/HR/5, Sales N°: E.87.XIV.2. Contains a list of countries which have ratified 22 human rights instruments of the United Nations system and includes the declarations and reservations presented by each country up to 1987. Every six months the list of ratifications is updated. The most recent version we have been able to consult is document ST/HR/4/Rev.12.

Multilateral Treaties Deposited with the Secretary-General: ST/LEG/SER.E/11, Sales N° F.93.V.11 (in French) and E.93.V.11 (in English). This contains a list of countries which have ratified each instrument, up to 31st December 1993, and the text of the declarations and reservations presented by the States on ratification of each instrument.

Documentation produced by the Human Rights Committee:
The annual reports of the Human Rights Committee to the General Assembly are issued as supplements to the Official Records of the General Assembly (CCPR/5, formerly entitled *United Nations Yearbook*

of the Human Rights Committee). Selected Decisions of the Human Rights Committee Under the Optional Protocol is published as document CCPR/C/OP/2.

4. Brief consultative bibliography on human rights and international organizations

COULTER, Robert,
1984   *The Evolution of International Human Rights Standards: Implications for Indigenous Peoples.* Washington, Indian Law Resource Center.
BERNHARDT, Rudolf (ed.),
1985   *Encyclopedia of Public International Law*, vol. 8 "Human Rights and the individual in International Law". Amsterdam/ N.York/Oxford, Elsevier Science Publ.
HANNUM, Hurst (ed.),
        Guide to International Human Rights Practice. London Macmillan Press.
HANNUM, Hurst,
1990   *Autonomy, Sovereignty and Self-Determination: the accommodation of conflicting rights.* Philadelphia, Univ. of Pennsylvania Press.
INDIAN LAW RESOURCE CENTER
1988   *Indian Rights, Human Rights. Handbook for Indians on International Human Rights Complaint Procedures.* Washington, ILRC, (2nd. printing).
MINNESOTA ADVOCATES FOR HUMAN RIGHTS/INTERNATIONAL SERVICE FOR HUMAN RIGHTS
1993   *Orientation Manual. The UN Commission on Human Rights, its Sub-Commission, and related procedures.* Minneapolis, MAHR/ISHR.
O'DONNELL, Daniel,
1988   *Protección internacional de los derechos humanos.* Lima, Andean Commission of Jurists/Friedrich Naumann Foundation.
PRÉMONT, Daniel; SANTOS PAIS, Marta y Liliana VALIÑA
1992   *Términos y conceptos relativos a los derechos humanos, los derechos de la mujer y del niño.* Geneva, CIFEDHOP
VALIÑA, Liliana,
1998   *"La evolución de las normas y mecanismos internacionales de derechos humanos en las Naciones Unidas"*, in *Lecciones y Ensayos* n° 68, Aug/Sept. 1998, Buenos Aires, Faculty of Law and Social Sciences, UBA.
Van de FLIERT, Lydia (comp.),
1897   *Guía para pueblos indígenas. Sobre políticas, proyectos, asistencia financiera y técnica de Agencias Internacionales, Gubernamentales y no Gubernamentales en América Latina.* Mexico, National Commission for Human Rights.

VASAK, Karel (ed.),
1982   *The International Dimensions of Human Rights*. Westport, UNESCO/ Greenwood Press, 2 vols.

ANNEX N° 1

INDIGENOUS ORGANIZATIONS IN CONSULTATIVE STATUS WITH THE UNITED NATIONS ECONOMIC AND SOCIAL COUNCIL (ECOSOC)

- *Aboriginal and Torres Strait Islander Commission (ATSIC)*
  MLC Tower, Woden Square, P.O. Box 17, WODEN
  ACT 2606, AUSTRALIA
  Tel: (11 61) 62-893420
  Fax: (11 61) 62-853603

- *Asociación Kunas Unidos por Napguana*
  Av. Justo Arosemena, Calle 41, casa 3-88
  Panamá, PANAMA
  Tel: (507) 25-4105
  Fax: (507) 227-5886
  e-mail: napguana@pty.com
  Internet: http://napguana.home.ml.org

- *Four Directions Council*
  Native American St., Univ. of Lethbridge,
  Lethbridge, Alberta
  T1K 3M4, CANADA
  Tel: (1 403) 329-2635
  Fax: (1 403) 380-1855
  e-mail: barsh@hg.uleth.ca

- *Grand Council of the Cree*
  2 Lakeshore Rd., Nemaska, Quebec
  J0Y 3B0, CANADA
  Tel: (1819) 673-2600
  Fax: (1819) 673-2606

- *Consejo Indio de Sud América / Indian Council of South America*
  Av. Simón Bolívar
  1512, Puno, PERU
  Tel/fax: (51 54) 35-5362
  e-mail: tcondori@puebloIndio.com
  Internet: http://www.puebloIndio.org/CISA/

- *Indian Law Resource Centre (ILRC)*
  508 Stuart Street, Helena
  Montana 59601, UNITED STATES OF AMERICA
  Tel: (1406) 449-2006
  Fax: (1406) 449-2031
  Internet: http://www.indianlaw.org
  Office in Washington:
  601 E Street, Southeast,
  Washington DC 20003, UNITED STATES OF AMERICA
  Tel: (1202) 547-2800
  Fax: (1202) 547-2803

- *Indigenous World Association*
  275 Grand View Ave., # 204, San Francisco,
  California, CA 94114, UNITED STATES OF AMERICA
  Tel: (1415) 647-1966

- *International Indian Treaty Council (IITC)*
  54 Mint Street, # 400
  San Francisco, California
  CA , 94103, UNITED STATES OF AMERICA
  Tel: (1 415) 512-1501
  Fax: (1 415) 512-1507
  e-mail: iitc@igc.apc.org

- *International Organization of Indigenous Resource Development*
  P.O. Box 219, Hobbema, Alberta
  T0C 1N0, CANADA
  Tel: (1 403) 585-3741
  Fax: (1 403) 585-2550

- *Inuit Circumpolar Conference (ICC)*
  P.O. Box 204, Nuuk
  3900, GREENLAND
  Tel: (299) 23-632
  Fax: (299) 23-001
  e-mail: iccgreen@greenet.gl

- *National Aboriginal and Islander Legal Services Secretariat (NAILSS)*
  Suite 2501, Level 25, MLC Centre
  239 George Street, P.O. Box 366, Roma Street, Brisbane
  4003, AUSTRALIA
  Tel: (61 7) 3211-3522
  Fax: (61 7) 3211-3234

- *National Indian Youth Council*
  318 Elm Street, Southeast, Albuquerque
  New Mexico 87102, UNITED STATES OF AMERICA
  Tel: (1505) 247-2251
  Fax: (1505) 247-4251

- *Saami Councili*
  Ohcejohka, Utsjoki
  SF-99980, FINLAND
  Tel: (358 16) 677-351
  Fax: (358 16) 677-353

  P.O. Box 200
  S-96225 Jokkmokk
  SUECIA
  Tel: (46 97) 11-2408
  Fax: (46 97) 11-2637
  e-mail: ssr@sapmi.se

- *Treaty Four*
  P.O. Box 985, Fort Qu'Appelle
  Saskatchewan, CANADA
  Tel: (1 306) 332-1874
  Fax: (1 306) 332-1811

- *World Council of Indigenous Peoples (WCIP)*
  Building 347, Croil Street, Ottawa, Ontario
  K1V 1J4, CANADA
  Tel: (1 613) 990-1114
  Fax: (1 613) 990-5038

ANNEX N° 2

LIST OF NON-INDIGENOUS NGOs WHICH MAY SUPPORT INDIGENOUS CAUSES AND PROJECTS

NAME AND ADDRESS	AIMS AND ACTIVITIES
Amnesty International (AI) 1 Easton Street, London WC1X 8DJ UNITED KINGDOM Tel: (44 171) 413-5500 Fax: (44 171) 956-1157 Email: amnesty@gn.apc.org	To achieve the abolition of the death penalty, the liberation of political prisoners and an end to torture and execution throughout the world. AI organizes campaigns to put pressure on governments which violate human rights, it launches urgent actions on behalf of victims, sends investigation teams to different countries and prepares annual reports on the situation of human rights around the world.
Anti-Slavery International Thomas Clarkson House The Stableyard, Broomgrove Road, London SW9 9TL. UNITED KINGDOM Tel: (44 171) 924-9555 Fax: (44 171) 738-4110 Email: antislavery@gn.apc.org Web site: http://www.charitynet.org/~asi	To promote the eradication of all forms of slavery and the liberation of all persons subjected to these types of practices, in particular amongst the most vulnerable groups: women, children, migrant workers and indigenous peoples. To collect and publicly disseminate information regarding these abuses; to identify and propose measures for preventing them; to support victims in their fight for freedom.
ARIS **(Anti-Racism Information Service)** 14, Av. Trembley 1209 Geneva SWITZERLAND Tel: (41 22) 740-3530 Fax (41 22) 740-3565 Email: aris@geneva-link.ch	To make known the Convention on Racial Discrimination and the work of the CERD; to provide a service to NGOs not represented in the UN, providing them with official documentation, assistance and information.

Defence for Children International 1 rue de Varembé, PO Box 88, 1211 Geneva 20 SWITZERLAND Tel: (41 22) 734-0558 Fax: (41 22) 740 -1145 Email: dci-hq@pingnet.ch Web site: http://www.chidhub.ch/webpub/dcihome	To promote and protect the rights of children by supervising application of the Convention on the Rights of the Child and through other research and investigation, information, campaigning and training activities.
DoCip (Indigenous Peoples' Centre for Documentation, Research and Information) 14, Av. Trembley 1209 Geneva SWITZERLAND Tel: (41 22) 740-3433 Fax: (41 22) 740-3454 Email: docip@iprolink.ch Web site: http://www.docip.org	To facilitate the links between indigenous peoples and the UN, providing support and technical assistance to indigenous delegates during the meetings in Geneva; to act as a liaison between indigenous organizations; to collect, archive and distribute documentation on international organizations and indigenous peoples. It regularly publishes an *Update* reporting on the main UN meetings of interest to indigenous peoples.
Human Rights Internet (HRI) Human Rights Centre, University of Ottawa, 57 Louis Pasteur, Ottawa, Ontario K1N 6N5 CANADA Tel: (16 13) 564-3492 Fax: (16 13) 564-4054	To encourage education and research in the field of human rights and to promote the formation of international solidarity networks. HRI has set up a documentation centre and a databank which is at the disposal of researchers and activists in the area of human rights.
International Commission of Jurists PO Box 216, 81A, Avenue de Châtelaine, 1219 Geneva SWITZERLAND Tel: (41 22) 797-3800 Fax: (41 22) 797-3801 Email: info@icj.org	To promote understanding and respect for the rule of law, as well as the legal protection of human rights throughout the world; to protect the independence of judicial power. The ICJ contributes to the human rights standar-setting process, denounces violations of those rights, and provides technical assistance to governments, as well as activists and groups requiring protection. It publishes a Year Book, a twice yearly journal and a quarterly bulletin.

IWGIA (International Work Group for Indigenous Affairs) Fioldstraede 10, DK-1171, Copenhagen K, DENMARK Tel: (45) 33 12 47 24 Fax: (45) 33 14 77 48 E-mail: iwgia@iwgia.org	To overcome racism and ensure respect for the rights of indigenous peoples, in particular the right to self-determination. To support projects which promote the social, cultural and political situation of indigenous peoples. To disseminate information on indigenous peoples (Year Book, bulletins and a Documents series)
Minority Rights Group 379 Brixton Road, London SW9 7DE UNITED KINGDOM Tel: (44 171) 978 9498 Fax: (44 171) 1738 6265 E-mail: minority.rights@mrg.sprinz.com	To ensure justice for discriminated minority groups and to achieve peaceful coexistence between minorities and the majority. Dissemination activities around minority groups (publication of research, conference reports, books, occasional documents, a quarterly bulletin and the *World Directory of Minorities*); defence of the rights of minorities within international fora and with governments; the development of local scale projects which improve the living conditions of minorities.
Survival International 11-15 Emerald Street London WC1N 3QL UNITED KINGDOM Tel: (44 171) 242-1441 Fax: (44 171) 242 -1771 E-mail: survival@gn.apc.org	To help indigenous peoples to protect their rights, in particular with regard to land, providing information on the outside world and giving international publicity to their problems and aspirations. It supports projects in the field with threatened groups, especially in Latin America, and publishes a quarterly Journal and a series of Documents.
Women's International League for Peace and Freedom 1 rue de Varembé PO Box 28, CH 1211 Geneva SWITZERLAND Tel: (41 22) 733-6175 Fax: (41 22) 740-1063 Email: wilpf@iprolink.ch	To unite determined women around the abolition of the political, social, economic and psychological causes of war. Educational, informational and mobilising activities for disarmament, peace, social justice, respect for human rights, the promotion of women and the elimination of racism.

World Council of Churches 150 route de Ferney, P O Box 2100, 1211 Geneva 2 SWITZERLAND Tel: (4122) 791-6111 Fax: (41 22) 791-0361 Web site: http://wcc-coe.org/wcc/contact/html	To promote the unity of the churches so that they become an instrument for peace, justice and strengthening of links between peoples. It has a programme on Indigenous Peoples and Land Rights and, since 1995, an indigenous consultant who works in this area.
World Organization against Torture PO Box 119 37-39, rue de Vermont 1211, Geneva 20 SWITZERLAND Tel: (41 22) 733-3140 Fax: (41 22) 733-1051 Email: omct@iprolink.ch Web site: http://www.omct.org	To help victims of torture, of forced disappearances, of summary executions and other forms of serious violence, immediately disseminating all viable information to national and international authorities likely to prevent this kind of crimes. It provides financial support to victims of torture, to be used on medical, social and/or legal assistance.

ANNEX N° 3
HOW TO OBTAIN CONSULTATIVE STATUS WITH ECOSOC

Resolution 1296 (XLIV) of the Economic and Social Council, approved on the 23rd May 1968, indicates the conditions under which a non-governmental organization may apply for consultative status with ECOSOC and for what type of consultation this may be used. In this Annex, we include the parts of this resolution which may be of use to any non-governmental organization wishing to initiate this process. The elements we consider to be of most importance are highlighted in bold. Parts of the resolution not reproduced here are indicated thus [...].

[...]

ARRANGEMENTS FOR CONSULTATION WITH NON-GOVERNMENTAL ORGANIZATIONS

Part I

Principles to be applied in the establishment of consultative relations

The following principles shall be applied in establishing consultative relations with non-governmental organizations

1. The organization shall be concerned with matters falling within the competence of the Economic and Social Council with respect to international economic, social, cultural, educational, health, scientific, technological **and related matters and to questions of human rights**.

2. The aims and purposes of the organization shall be in conformity with the spirit, purposes and principles of the Charter of the United Nations.

3. The organization shall undertake to support the work of the United Nations and to promote knowledge of its principles and activities. [...]

4. **The organization shall be of representative character and of recognized international standing**; it shall represent a substantial proportion, and express the views of major sections, of the population or of the organized persons within the particular field of its competence, covering, where possible, a substantial number of countries in different regions of the world. [...]

5. **The organization shall have an established headquarters, with an executive officer**. It shall have a **democratically adopted constitution**, a copy of which shall be deposited with the Secretary-General of the United Nations, and which shall provide for the determination of policy by a conference, congress or other representative body, and for an executive organ responsible to the policy-making body.

6. **The organization shall have authority to speak for its members through its authorized representatives.** [...]

7. Subject to paragraph 9 below, **the organization shall be international in its structure**, **with members who exercise voting rights** in relation to the policies or action of the international organization. Any international organization which is not established by intergovernmental agreement shall be considered as a non-governmental organization for the purpose of these arrangements. [...]

8. **The basic resources of the international organization shall be derived in the main part from contributions of the national affiliates or other components or from individual members**. Where voluntary contributions have been received, their amounts and donors shall be faithfully revealed to the Council Committee on Non-Governmental Organizations. [...]

9. National organizations shall normally present their views through international non-governmental organizations to which they belong. **It would not, save in exceptional cases, be appropriate to admit national organizations which are affiliated to an international non-governmental organization covering the same subjects on an international basis.**[...]

10. Consultative arrangements shall not normally be made with an international organization which is a member of a committee or group composed of international organizations with which consultative arrangements have been made.

11. In considering the establishment of consultative relations with a non-governmental organization, the Council will take into account

whether the field of activity of the organization is wholly or mainly within the field of a specialized agency, and whether or not it could be admitted when it has, or may have, a consultative arrangement with a specialized agency.

Part II

Principles governing the nature of the consultative arrangements

12. A clear distinction is drawn in the Charter of the United Nations between participation without vote in the deliberations of the Council and the arrangements for consultation. [...] **This distinction, deliberately made in the Charter, is fundamental and the arrangements for consultation should not be such as to accord to non-governmental organizations the same rights of participation as are accorded to States not members of the Council and to the specialized agencies brought into relationship with the United Nations.** [...]

14. [...] The arrangements for consultation made with each organization **should involve only the subjects for which that organization has a special competence or in which it has a special interest.** [...]

Part III

Establishment of consultative relationships

15. In establishing consultative relationships with each organization, regard shall be had to the nature and scope of its activities and to the assistance it may be expected to give to the Council or its subsidiary bodies [...]

16. In establishing consultative relations with organizations, **the Council will distinguish between:**

   a) Organizations which are concerned with most of the activities of the Council and can demonstrate to the satisfaction of the Council that they have marked and sustained contributions to make to the achievement of the objectives of the United Nations in the fields [within their competence]. [Such organizations][...] will be known as **organizations in general consultative status, category I)**;

   b) Organizations which have a special competence in, and are concerned specifically with, only a few the fields of activity covered by the Council, which are known internationally within the fields for which they have or seek consultative status (**to be known as organizations** in **special consultative status, category II**).

17. Organizations accorded consultative status in category II because of their interest in the field of human rights should have a general international concern with this matter, not restricted to the interests of a particular group of persons, a single nationality of the situation in a single State or restricted group of States. [...]

19. **Other organizations which** do not have general or special consultative status but which the Council, or the Secretary-General of the United Nations, [...] considers **can make occasional and useful contributions** to the work of the Council or its subsidiary bodies or other United Nations bodies within their competence **shall be included in a list (to be known as the Roster)**. [...] These organizations shall be available for consultation at the request of the Council or its subsidiary bodies. The fact that an organization is on the Roster shall not in itself be regarded as a qualification for general or special consultative should an organization seek such status.

Part IV

Consultation with the Council

Provisional agenda

20. The provisional agenda of the Council shall be communicated to organizations in categories I and II and to those on the Roster.

21. **Organizations in category I** may propose to the Council Committee on Non-Governmental Organizations that the Committee request the Secretary-General to place **items of special interest** to the organizations on the provisional agenda of the Council.

Attendance at meetings

22. **Organizations in categories I and II** may designate authorized representatives to sit as observers at public meetings of the Council and its subsidiary bodies. Those on the Roster may have representatives present at such meetings concerned with matters within their field of competence.

[...]

ANNEX N° 4
THE UNITED NATIONS DRAFT DECLARATION ON THE RIGHTS OF INDIGENOUS PEOPLES APPROVED BY THE WGIP IN 1994[1]

Affirming that indigenous peoples are equal in dignity and rights to all other peoples, while recognizing the right of all peoples to be different, to consider themselves different, and to be respected as such,

Affirming also that all peoples contribute to the diversity and richness of civilizations and cultures, which constitute the common heritage of humankind,

Affirming further that all doctrines, policies and practices based on or advocating superiority of peoples or individuals on the basis of national origin, racial, religious, ethnic or cultural differences are racist, scientifically false, legally invalid, morally condemnable and socially unjust,

Reaffirming also that indigenous peoples, in the exercise of their rights, should be free from discrimination of any kind,

Concerned that indigenous peoples have been deprived of their human rights and fundamental freedoms, resulting, inter alia, in their colonization and dispossession of their lands, territories and resources, thus preventing them from exercising, in particular, their right to development in accordance with their own needs and interests,

Recognizing the urgent need to respect and promote the inherent rights and characteristics of indigenous peoples, especially their rights to their lands, territories and resources, which derive from their political, economic and social structures and from their cultures, spiritual traditions, histories and philosophies,

Welcoming the fact that indigenous peoples are organizing themselves for political, economic, social and cultural enhancement and in order to bring an end to all forms of discrimination and oppression wherever they occur,

Convinced that control by indigenous peoples over developments affecting them and their lands, territories and resources will enable them to maintain and strengthen their institutions, cultures and traditions, and to promote their development in accordance with their aspirations and needs,

Recognizing also that respect for indigenous knowledge, cultures and traditional practices contributes to sustainable and equitable development and proper management of the environment,

Emphasizing the need for demilitarization of the lands and territories of indigenous peoples, which will contribute to peace, economic and social progress and development, understanding and friendly relations among nations and peoples of the world,

Recognizing in particular the right of indigenous families and communities to retain shared responsibility for the upbringing, training, education and well-being of their children,

Recognizing also that indigenous peoples have the right freely to determine their relationships with States in a spirit of coexistence, mutual benefit and full respect,

Considering that treaties, agreements and other arrangements between States and indigenous peoples are properly matters of international concern and responsibility,

Acknowledging that the Charter of the United Nations, the International Covenant on Economic, Social and Cultural Rights and the International Covenant on Civil and Political Rights affirm the fundamental importance of the right of self-determination of all peoples, by virtue of which they freely determine their political status and freely pursue their economic, social and cultural development,

Bearing in mind that nothing in this Declaration may be used to deny any peoples their right of self-determination,

Encouraging States to comply with and effectively implement all international instruments, in particular those related to human rights, as they apply to indigenous peoples, in consultation and cooperation with the peoples concerned,

Emphasizing that the United Nations has an important and continuing role to play in promoting and protecting the rights of indigenous peoples,

Believing that this Declaration is a further important step forward for the recognition, promotion and protection of the rights and freedoms of indigenous peoples and in the development of relevant activities of the United Nations system in this field,

Solemnly proclaims the following United Nations Declaration on the Rights of Indigenous Peoples:

PART I

Article 1
Indigenous peoples have the right to the full and effective enjoyment of all human rights and fundamental freedoms recognized in the Charter of the United Nations, the Universal Declaration of Human Rights and international human rights law.

Article 2
Indigenous individuals and peoples are free and equal to all other individuals and peoples in dignity and rights, and have the right to be free from any kind of adverse discrimination, in particular that based on their indigenous origin or identity.

Article 3
Indigenous peoples have the right of self-determination. By virtue of that right they freely determine their political status and freely pursue their economic, social and cultural development.

Article 4
Indigenous peoples have the right to maintain and strengthen their distinct political, economic, social and cultural characteristics, as well as their legal systems, while retaining their rights to participate fully, if they so choose, in the political, economic, social and cultural life of the State.

Article 5
Every indigenous individual has the right to a nationality.

PART II

Article 6
Indigenous peoples have the collective right to live in freedom, peace and security as distinct peoples and to full guarantees against genocide or any other act of violence, including the removal of indigenous

children from their families and communities under any pretext.
In addition, they have the individual rights to life, physical and mental integrity, liberty and security of person.

Article 7
Indigenous peoples have the collective and individual right not to be subjected to ethnocide and cultural genocide, including prevention of and redress for:
    a) Any action which has the aim or effect of depriving them of their integrity as distinct peoples, or of their cultural values or ethnic identities;
    b) Any action which has the aim or effect of dispossessing them of their lands, territories or resources;
    c) Any form of population transfer which has the aim or effect of violating or undermining any of their rights;
    d) Any form of assimilation or integration by other cultures or ways of life imposed on them by legislative, administrative or other measures;
    e) Any form of propaganda directed against them.

Article 8
Indigenous peoples have the collective and individual right to maintain and develop their distinct identities and characteristics, including the right to identify themselves as indigenous and to be recognized as such.

Article 9
Indigenous peoples and individuals have the right to belong to an indigenous community or nation, in accordance with the traditions and customs of the community or nation concerned. No disadvantage of any kind may arise from the exercise of such a right.

Article 10
Indigenous peoples shall not be forcibly removed from their lands or territories. No relocation shall take place without the free and informed consent of the indigenous peoples concerned and after agreement on just and fair compensation and, where possible, with the option of return.

Article 11
Indigenous peoples have the right to special protection and security in periods of armed conflict.
    States shall observe international standards, in particular the Fourth Geneva Convention of 1949, for the protection of civilian populations in circumstances of emergency and armed conflict, and shall not:

a) Recruit indigenous individuals against their will into the armed forces and, in particular, for use against other indigenous peoples;
b) Recruit indigenous children into the armed forces under any circumstances;
c) Force indigenous individuals to abandon their lands, territories or means of subsistence, or relocate them in special centres for military purposes;
d) Force indigenous individuals to work for military purposes under any discriminatory conditions.

PART III

Article 12
Indigenous peoples have the right to practise and revitalize their cultural traditions and customs. This includes the right to maintain, protect and develop the past, present and future manifestations of their cultures, such as archaeological and historical sites, artifacts, designs, ceremonies, technologies and visual and performing arts and literature, as well as the right to the restitution of cultural, intellectual, religious and spiritual property taken without their free and informed consent or in violation of their laws, traditions and customs.

Article 13
Indigenous peoples have the right to manifest, practise, develop and teach their spiritual and religious traditions, customs and ceremonies; the right to maintain, protect, and have access in privacy to their religious and cultural sites; the right to the use and control of ceremonial objects; and the right to the repatriation of human remains.
 States shall take effective measures, in conjunction with the indigenous peoples concerned, to ensure that indigenous sacred places, including burial sites, be preserved, respected and protected.

Article 14
Indigenous peoples have the right to revitalize, use, develop and transmit to future generations their histories, languages, oral traditions, philosophies, writing systems and literatures, and to designate and retain their own names for communities, places and persons.
 States shall take effective measures, whenever any right of indigenous peoples may be threatened, to ensure this right is protected and also to ensure that they can understand and be understood in political, legal and administrative proceedings, where necessary through the provision of interpretation or by other appropriate means.

PART IV

Article 15
Indigenous children have the right to all levels and forms of education of the State. All indigenous peoples also have this right and the right to establish and control their educational systems and institutions providing education in their own languages, in a manner appropriate to their cultural methods of teaching and learning.

Indigenous children living outside their communities have the right to be provided access to education in their own culture and language. States shall take effective measures to provide appropriate resources for these purposes.

Article 16
Indigenous peoples have the right to have the dignity and diversity of their cultures, traditions, histories and aspirations appropriately reflected in all forms of education and public information.

States shall take effective measures, in consultation with the indigenous peoples concerned, to eliminate prejudice and discrimination and to promote tolerance, understanding and good relations among indigenous peoples and all segments of society.

Article 17
Indigenous peoples have the right to establish their own media in their own languages. They also have the right to equal access to all forms of non-indigenous media.

States shall take effective measures to ensure that State-owned media duly reflect indigenous cultural diversity.

Article 18
Indigenous peoples have the right to enjoy fully all rights established under international labour law and national labour legislation. Indigenous individuals have the right not to be subjected to any discriminatory conditions of labour, employment or salary.

PART V

Article 19
Indigenous peoples have the right to participate fully, if they so choose, at all levels of decision-making in matters which may affect their rights, lives and destinies through representatives chosen by themselves in accordance with their own procedures, as well as to maintain and develop their own indigenous decision-making institutions.

Article 20
Indigenous peoples have the right to participate fully, if they so choose, through procedures determined by them, in devising legislative or administrative measures that may affect them.
  States shall obtain the free and informed consent of the peoples concerned before adopting and implementing such measures.

Article 21
Indigenous peoples have the right to maintain and develop their political, economic and social systems, to be secure in the enjoyment of their own means of subsistence and development, and to engage freely in all their traditional and other economic activities. Indigenous peoples who have been deprived of their means of subsistence and development are entitled to just and fair compensation.

Article 22
Indigenous peoples have the right to special measures for the immediate, effective and continuing improvement of their economic and social conditions, including in the areas of employment, vocational training and retraining, housing, sanitation, health and social security.
Particular attention shall be paid to the rights and special needs of indigenous elders, women, youth, children and disabled persons.

Article 23
Indigenous peoples have the right to determine and develop priorities and strategies for exercising their right to development. In particular, indigenous peoples have the right to determine and develop all health, housing and other economic and social programmes affecting them and, as far as possible, to administer such programmes through their own institutions.

Article 24
Indigenous peoples have the right to their traditional medicines and health practices, including the right to the protection of vital medicinal plants, animals and minerals.
  They also have the right to access, without any discrimination, to all medical institutions, health services and medical care.

PART VI

Article 25
Indigenous peoples have the right to maintain and strengthen their distinctive spiritual and material relationship with the lands, territo-

ries, waters and coastal seas and other resources which they have traditionally owned or otherwise occupied or used, and to uphold their responsibilities to future generations in this regard.

Article 26
Indigenous peoples have the right to own, develop, control and use the lands and territories, including the total environment of the lands, air, waters, coastal seas, sea-ice, flora and fauna and other resources which they have traditionally owned or otherwise occupied or used. This includes the right to the full recognition of their laws, traditions and customs, land-tenure systems and institutions for the development and management of resources, and the right to effective measures by States to prevent any interference with, alienation of or encroachment upon these rights.

Article 27
Indigenous peoples have the right to the restitution of the lands, territories and resources which they have traditionally owned or otherwise occupied or used, and which have been confiscated, occupied, used or damaged without their free and informed consent. Where this is not possible, they have the right to just and fair compensation. Unless otherwise freely agreed upon by the peoples concerned, compensation shall take the form of lands, territories and resources equal in quality, size and legal status.

Article 28
Indigenous peoples have the right to the conservation, restoration and protection of the total environment and the productive capacity of their lands, territories and resources, as well as to assistance for this purpose from States and through international cooperation. Military activities shall not take place in the lands and territories of indigenous peoples, unless otherwise freely agreed upon by the peoples concerned.
 States shall take effective measures to ensure that no storage or disposal of hazardous materials shall take place in the lands and territories of indigenous peoples.
 States shall also take effective measures to ensure, as needed, that programmes for monitoring, maintaining and restoring the health of indigenous peoples, as developed and implemented by the peoples affected by such materials, are duly implemented.

Article 29
Indigenous peoples are entitled to the recognition of the full ownership, control and protection of their cultural and intellectual property. They have the right to special measures to control, develop and protect

their sciences, technologies and cultural manifestations, including human and other genetic resources, seeds, medicines, knowledge of the properties of fauna and flora, oral traditions, literatures, designs and visual and performing arts.

Article 30
Indigenous peoples have the right to determine and develop priorities and strategies for the development or use of their lands, territories and other resources, including the right to require that States obtain their free and informed consent prior to the approval of any project affecting their lands, territories and other resources, particularly in connection with the development, utilization or exploitation of mineral, water or other resources. Pursuant to agreement with the indigenous peoples concerned, just and fair compensation shall be provided for any such activities and measures taken to mitigate adverse environmental, economic, social, cultural or spiritual impact.

PART VII

Article 31
Indigenous peoples, as a specific form of exercising their right to self-determination, have the right to autonomy or self-government in matters relating to their internal and local affairs, including culture, religion, education, information, media, health, housing, employment, social welfare, economic activities, land and resources management, environment and entry by non-members, as well as ways and means for financing these autonomous functions.

Article 32
Indigenous peoples have the collective right to determine their own citizenship in accordance with their customs and traditions. Indigenous citizenship does not impair the right of indigenous individuals to obtain citizenship of the States in which they live.
    Indigenous peoples have the right to determine the structures and to select the membership of their institutions in accordance with their own procedures.

Article 33
Indigenous peoples have the right to promote, develop and maintain their institutional structures and their distinctive juridical customs, traditions, procedures and practices, in accordance with internationally recognized human rights standards.

Article 34
Indigenous peoples have the collective right to determine the responsibilities of individuals to their communities.

Article 35
Indigenous peoples, in particular those divided by international borders, have the right to maintain and develop contacts, relations and cooperation, including activities for spiritual, cultural, political, economic and social purposes, with other peoples across borders.
    States shall take effective measures to ensure the exercise and implementation of this right.

Article 36
Indigenous peoples have the right to the recognition, observance and enforcement of treaties, agreements and other constructive arrangements concluded with States or their successors, according to their original spirit and intent, and to have States honour and respect such treaties, agreements and other constructive arrangements. Conflicts and disputes which cannot otherwise be settled should be submitted to competent international bodies agreed to by all parties concerned.

PART VIII

Article 37
States shall take effective and appropriate measures, in consultation with the indigenous peoples concerned, to give full effect to the provisions of this Declaration. The rights recognized herein shall be adopted and included in national legislation in such a manner that indigenous peoples can avail themselves of such rights in practice.

Article 38
Indigenous peoples have the right to have access to adequate financial and technical assistance, from States and through international cooperation, to pursue freely their political, economic, social, cultural and spiritual development and for the enjoyment of the rights and freedoms recognized in this Declaration.

Article 39
Indigenous peoples have the right to have access to and prompt decision through mutually acceptable and fair procedures for the resolution of conflicts and disputes with States, as well as to effective remedies for all infringements of their individual and collective rights.

Such a decision shall take into consideration the customs, traditions, rules and legal systems of the indigenous peoples concerned.

Article 40
The organs and specialized agencies of the United Nations system and other intergovernmental organizations shall contribute to the full realization of the provisions of this Declaration through the mobilization, inter alia, of financial cooperation and technical assistance. Ways and means of ensuring participation of indigenous peoples on issues affecting them shall be established.

Article 41
The United Nations shall take the necessary steps to ensure the implementation of this Declaration including the creation of a body at the highest level with special competence in this field and with the direct participation of indigenous peoples. All United Nations bodies shall promote respect for and full application of the provisions of this Declaration.

PART IX

Article 42
The rights recognized herein constitute the minimum standards for the survival, dignity and well-being of the indigenous peoples of the world.

Article 43
All the rights and freedoms recognized herein are equally guaranteed to male and female indigenous individuals.

Article 44
Nothing in this Declaration may be construed as diminishing or extinguishing existing or future rights indigenous peoples may have or acquire.

Article 45
Nothing in this Declaration may be interpreted as implying for any State, group or person any right to engage in any activity or to perform any act contrary to the Charter of the United Nations.

Note

[1] As approved unanimously by the Sub-Commission on Prevention of Discrimination and Protection of Minorities in 1994 (Doc. E/CN.4/Sub.2/1994/2/Add.1).

ANNEX N° 5
INDIGENOUS DECLARATIONS REGARDING THE ESTABLISHMENT OF A PERMANENT FORUM FOR INDIGENOUS PEOPLES WITHIN THE UNITED NATIONS

Towards the end of the 1980s, some of the indigenous representatives who were participating in the meetings of the Working Group on Indigenous Populations began proposing the creation of a permanent forum devoted to indigenous issues, placed at the highest possible level within the hierarchy of the UNO. This idea arose from the simple fact that the aforementioned Working Group is an organ situated at the lowest level, which limits its decision making capacity enormously.

This suggestion was supported by the World Conference of Human Rights and by the General Assembly in 1993; in 1994 it was promoted by the Commission on Human Rights and the Working Group on Indigenous Populations. At the end of the following year, a report of the Secretary-General of the UNO confirmed that there still existed no mechanism within the United Nations system which enabled indigenous peoples to actively participate in its organs and to dialogue directly with governments and specialized agencies. The Government of Denmark, in association with the autonomous Government of Greenland, organized an initial seminar on the subject in 1995, followed by a second meeting in Santiago de Chile in 1997, sponsored by the authorities of this country. As a result of these consultations, in March 1998 the Commission on Human Rights decided to create a working group with the aim of formulating and considering proposals on the possible establishment of the said permanent forum, taking into consideration the reports of both seminars and comments received from governments, from the different organs of the UNO system and from indigenous organizations.

Alongside these government initiatives, indigenous peoples and organizations declared the need to meet amongst themselves at a regional level in order to gain information and formulate and discuss proposals concerning the establishment of a permanent forum. Apart from designing strategies for common action, the aim of these regional meetings was to facilitate the participation of indigenous organizations which are not working on an international level but which fight on a daily basis for their rights at a local and regional level. It is thus a question of opening up a dialogue between regional level indigenous representatives as a first step towards the adoption of a common position on the issue in the face of the competent organs of the United Nations.

The first International Indigenous Conference on the Establishment of a Permanent Forum in the UNO took place in Temuco, Chile, from 6th to 9th May 1997. It was organized by the mapuche association "Consejo de Todas las Tierras". Participants in the Temuco Conference demanded the prompt establishment of the permanent forum at the highest level possible within the UNO structure, guaranteeing the right of indigenous peoples to participate fully and effectively under the same conditions as governments. Finally, it was agreed that the mandate of the new organ should be sufficiently broad to cover all areas of interest to indigenous peoples.

The second International Indigenous Conference on the Establishment of a Permanent Forum in the UNO was held in Ukupseni, Kuna Yala (Panama) from 4th to 6th March 1998 and was organized by the Asociación Napguana. Participants agreed that the permanent forum should report to ECOSOC directly and three issues were debated: the mandate and powers of the permanent forum, its structure and indigenous participation and relations between the Permanent Forum and the Working Group on Indigenous Populations.

From 23rd to 25th September 1998, the first Asian Indigenous Peoples' Workshop on a Permanent Forum for Indigenous Peoples in the United Nations was held in Indore (Madhya Pradesh). The participants of this seminar reiterated the need for the prompt establishment of a permanent forum for indigenous peoples at the highest level within the UNO system, with a broad mandate, and debated the issues of its composition and participation in the discussions of this forum, the need for a specific secretariat and the funding implications of these new organs.

There now follows the texts of the final declarations of each of these meetings:

Declaration of the "First International Indigenous Conference on the Establishment of a Permanent Forum in the United Nations"
Temuco, Chile, May 6-7, 1997

We, the indigenous peoples meeting in Temuco, reaffirm the principles and objectives of Article 1.2 of the Charter of the United Nations: to develop friendly relations among nations based on respect for the principle of equal rights and self-determination of peoples, and to take other appropriate measures to strengthen universal peace,

Bearing in mind the recommendations pertaining to indigenous people included in the Vienna Declaration and Programme of Action adopted by the World Conference on Human Rights (A/CONF.157/23), concerning the establishment of a permanent forum for indigenous people in the United Nations system,

Recalling also the recommendations of the United Nations Conference on Environment and Development as stated in article 22 of the Rio Declaration on Environment and Development and chapters 11 and 26 of Agenda 21 concerning indigenous people,

Further recalling General Assembly resolution 50/157 in which the establishment of a permanent forum for indigenous people in the United Nations system is pinpointed as one of the major objectives of the International Decade of the World's Indigenous People along with the adoption of a United Nations Declaration on the Rights of Indigenous Peoples,

Welcoming the Secretary-General's review of the existing mechanisms, procedures and programmes within the United Nations concerning indigenous peoples (A/51/493),

Considering the Secretary-General's conclusions in which he states that there are no mechanisms in the United Nations organizations which give the indigenous peoples an opportunity to take part in decision-making, nor any regular exchange of information among Governments, indigenous peoples and the United Nations system,

We, the indigenous peoples, declare that:

1 In accordance with the principle of dialogue between Governments and peoples we call for the rapid establishment of the permanent forum at the highest possible level;

2 The indigenous peoples have the right to full and effective participation in the permanent forum on an equal footing with Governments. It is also important that United Nations agencies, non-governmental organizations and independent experts should have the opportunity to take part in the discussions of the permanent forum when the parties so require;

3 The mandate of the permanent forum should be sufficiently broad and cover all areas which concern the indigenous peoples of the world, including cultural, civil, political, social and economic rights,

health, women, children, development, education, the environment, territories, human rights, the resolution of conflicts and the coordination of activities with the United Nations agencies in which the indigenous peoples are involved.

Declaration of the Second International Indigenous Conference on a Permanent Forum for Indigenous People
Ukupseni, Kuna Yala, Panama
4-6 March 1998

We, the representatives of the indigenous peoples meeting in Kuna Yala, Panama, from 4 to 6 March 1998,

Bearing in mind United Nations resolutions and declarations such as those on indigenous peoples in relation to the establishment of a permanent forum for indigenous people within the United Nations system:

Article 1.2 of the United Nations Charter, in which the United Nations reaffirms as its purpose the development of friendly relations among nations based on respect for the principle of equal rights and self-determination of peoples, and other appropriate measures to strengthen universal peace;

The Vienna Declaration and Programme of Action adopted by the World Conference on Human Rights (A/CONF.157/23), which mentioned the need for a permanent forum for indigenous peoples within the United Nations system;

Article 22 of the United Nations Conference on Environment and Development, the Rio Declaration on Environment and Development, and chapters 11 and 26 of Agenda 21 relating to indigenous people;

United Nations General Assembly resolution 50/157, in which the establishment of a permanent United Nations forum is identified as one of the important objectives of the International Decade of the World's Indigenous People;

The Secretary-General's review of the existing mechanisms, procedures and programmes within the United Nations concerning indigenous people, which concludes that there are no United Nations mechanisms that give indigenous people the opportunity to take part in decision-making, and that there is no regular exchange of information between governments, indigenous people and the United Nations system;

The Declaration of the First International Indigenous Conference on a Permanent Forum in the United Nations System, held in Temuco, Chile, from 6 to 9 May 1997;

The report of the first workshop on a permanent forum for indigenous people within the United Nations system, held in Copenhagen, Denmark, from 26 to 28 June 1995 in accordance with the Commission on Human Rights resolution 1995/30(E/CN.4/Sub.2/AC.4/1995/7);

The report of the second workshop on a permanent forum for indigenous people within the United Nations system, held in accordance with Commission on Human Rights resolution 1997/30 in Santiago, Chile, from 30 June to 2 July 1997 (E/CN.4/1998/11 and Add.1),

We call for the speedy establishment of a permanent forum for indigenous people within the United Nations system, reporting directly to the Economic and Social Council (ECOSOC) and having the following characteristics:

1. Mandate

Promotion of peace and prosperity for indigenous people;

All matters relating to indigenous people;

Coordination within the United Nations system of activities relating to indigenous people;

Guidance and advice to States, specialized agencies and other relevant bodies;

Dissemination of information on the conditions and needs of indigenous people;

Promotion of understanding between peoples with a view to facilitating the prevention and peaceful settlement of disputes;

Formulation of all recommendations on any issue affecting indigenous people;

Compliance with existing national and international norms;

Issuing of proposals for harmonizing norms or laws with international law in the area of indigenous issues.

2. Terms of Reference

The permanent forum's terms of reference should include: civil, political and social rights of indigenous people, cultural rights, human rights, lands and territories, environment, health, children, women, development, education, coordination of the activities of United Nations bodies relating or referring to indigenous people, biodiversity, constitutional reform with emphasis on recognition of the cultural diversity of States, conflict prevention, development of national legislation as regards the rights of indigenous people, right to life, impact of disasters caused by human activity on indigenous people, promotion of the world view of indigenous people, mechanism for monitoring the implementation of legislation relating to indigenous people, reconstitution of indigenous peoples, indigenous economy, natural resources, training on the United Nations system, examination of the legal diversity of countries where indigenous people live and the effect of this pluralism, the development of language in furtherance of rights of indigenous people instead of customary law or normative systems, the growing use of the death penalty, recovery of indigenous lore, ethnology, indigenous science and technology, indigenous people living in border regions, formulation of proposals for indigenous people living in national border zones to have freedom of movement across borders.

3. Composition

As indigenous people, we have the right to participate fully and actively in the permanent forum as equal partners with Governments. We propose that there should be an equal number of government and indigenous representatives. United Nations specialized agencies, non-governmental organizations and independent experts should have the opportunity to participate in the permanent forum's deliberations as observers without the right to vote.

The size of the membership should be left open, but we think that there should be between 5 and 10 indigenous representatives.

4. The relationship between the permanent forum and the Working Group on Indigenous Populations

We consider:

That the existing Working Group on Indigenous Populations has unique characteristics as regards the participation of indigenous people, unlike any other body within the system;

That the achievements of the Working Group on Indigenous Populations and the inter-sessional Working Group of the Commission on Human Rights have been, and are, fundamental to the indigenous movement and should therefore be taken into account in the discussion on the permanent forum;

That they are two different bodies of vital importance; they should therefore complement each other and one should not substitute for the other, which could result in strategies at variance with the indigenous movement;

That the Working Group on Indigenous Populations is a technical body, whereas the permanent forum is a political body, and therefore they are not in conflict with each other;

That the role of the Working Group is confined to the formulation of international norms for the protection of the human rights of indigenous people, while the role of the permanent forum is much broader, encompassing human rights among other matters;

That in the United Nations system there are examples of bodies which deal with the same issues such as the Committee on the Elimination of Discrimination against Women and the Committee against Torture. Therefore, the establishment of the forum and the simultaneous existence of the Working Group are not incompatible;

5. We conclude:

That the permanent forum and the Working Group are necessary and important platforms for our participation in the United Nations system, in order to apply the international provisions relating to our rights as indigenous people;

That the establishment of the permanent forum is an important objective as a political organ at the highest level which will permit our broad participation in the United Nations system in areas of concern to us;

That there should be a close relationship between the permanent forum and the fulfilment of the Working Group's mandate for the approval of the United Nations Declaration on the Rights of Indigenous Peoples and other issues of relevance to us as indigenous people;

That once the forum is established and its mandate and terms of reference decided, the mandate of the Working Group should be reviewed so that thelatter complements the mandate of the permanent forum;

That in pursuance of the Working Group's mandate, we as indigenous peoples should consolidate its effectiveness in the discussion of the topics of the United Nations Declaration on the Rights of Indigenous Peoples and ensure that the Group's work is relevant to the new needs of indigenous people;

That it is necessary to strengthen our participation in the Working Group in order to ensure the approval of the United Nations Declaration on the Rights of Indigenous People and the establishment of a permanent forum within the framework of the Decade;

That the Sub-Commission on Prevention of Discrimination and Protection of Minorities and the Commission on Human Rights should continue to entrust to the Working Group normative tasks and specific actions for the promotion and protection of the rights of indigenous people.

Ukupseni, Kuna Yala (Panama), 6 March 1998

First Asian Indigenous Peoples' Workshop On A Permanent Forum For Indigenous Peoples In The United Nations

Indore Declaration

We, the representatives of indigenous peoples meeting in Indore, Madhya Pradesh, India, from 23 to 25 September, 1998,

Bearing in mind the United Nation's resolutions and declarations pertaining to the rights of indigenous peoples, including those in relation to the establishment of a permanent forum for indigenous peoples within the UN system;

Recalling the rights of all peoples, including indigenous peoples, to self-determination as enshrined in the UN Charter;

Reiterating our demand for the early adoption of the Declaration on the Rights of Indigenous Peoples as adopted by the Sub-Commission on the Prevention of Discrimination and the Protection of Minorities;

Bearing in mind the Vienna Declaration and Programme of Action as adopted by the World Conference on Human Rights (A/CONF.157/23);

Recalling that the goal of the International Decade of the World's Indigenous Peoples is to strengthen international cooperation in order to solve problems faced by indigenous peoples in such areas as human rights, health, environment, development, education and culture;

Supporting the United Nations General Assembly Resolution 50/157 calling for the establishment of a permanent forum for indigenous peoples within the UN system as one of the important objectives of the International Decade of the World's Indigenous Peoples;

Recalling the Secretary General's Report on the Review of Existing Mechanisms, Procedures and Programmes within the United Nations concerning indigenous peoples (A/51/493);

Supporting the declarations coming from the first and second International Indigenous Peoples' Conferences on a Permanent Forum for Indigenous Peoples in the UN system held in Temuco, Chile (E/CN.4/1998/11/Add.1), and Kuna Yala, Panama (E/CN.4/1998/11/Add.3);

Recalling the reports from the first and second workshops on a Permanent Forum for Indigenous Peoples within the UN system held in Copenhagen, Denmark (E/CN.4/Sub.2/AC.4/1995/7) and Santiago de Chile (E/CN.4/1998/11);

Welcoming the decision of the Commission on Human Rights to establish an ad-hoc inter-sessional working group on the permanent forum;

Emphasizing the need for an indigenous co-chair for the ad-hoc inter-sessional working group on the permanent forum;

We call for the speedy establishment of a permanent forum for indigenous peoples within the UN system in order to facilitate dialogue between member states of the UN, indigenous peoples and UN bodies on issues and concerns affecting indigenous peoples.

Level:

The permanent forum should be at the highest level and no lower than a body reporting directly to the Economic and Social Council (ECOSOC) of the United Nations.

Mandate:

The mandate of the permanent forum should be as broad as possible and contain all matters concerning indigenous peoples amongst which should be included civil, political, economic, social, cultural, developmental, environmental, health, education, language, land, resources, territorial, gender and children's rights. In particular it should deal with the following, among others:

- To coordinate and monitor all activities of concern to indigenous peoples within and outside the UN system;

- To provide advice and guidance to member states of the UN, specialized agencies of the UN and other relevant bodies;

- To facilitate the establishment of national institutions and mechanisms on the rights of indigenous peoples;

- To conduct research into, and collect, provide and disseminate information on, the conditions and needs of indigenous peoples and on the UN institutions, agencies and related forums which concern indigenous peoples;

- To promote understanding between peoples with the aim of facilitating the prevention, and the peaceful resolution, of conflicts;

- To formulate recommendations on any issues of concern to indigenous peoples;

- To ensure the fulfilment of existing national and international standards with regard to the rights of indigenous peoples;

- To develop international standards on the rights of indigenous peoples;

- To take decisions for intervening effectively on an urgent basis on behalf of indigenous peoples throughout the world.

Membership, Composition and Participation

The forum should be composed of an equal number of representatives of indigenous peoples and member states of the UN, acting as full voting members on an equal basis. There should be at least two representatives of indigenous peoples from each of the main geographical regions around the world, to be nominated by indigenous peoples of the respective regions.

In addition, indigenous peoples and their organizations, member states of the UN, specialized agencies of the UN and non-governmental organizations, should be able to participate in the deliberations of the forum as observers without the right to vote. Indigenous peoples should have the same access to the forum as in the case of the Working Group on Indigenous Populations.

Secretariat

A new secretariat should be established for the permanent forum. This secretariat should be adequately staffed by qualified indigenous persons for the preparation and servicing of the permanent forum meetings and the collection and dissemination of information. The secretariat should also assist indigenous peoples in their capacity building efforts.

Finance

The funds for the functioning of the forum, its subsidiary bodies, including a secretariat, should be borne by the UN from its regular budget. Additionally, member states of the UN should be encouraged to contribute with voluntary funds and technical assistance.

INDEX OF KEY WORDS

Only the page on which the definition appears is mentioned, excluding places where the key word appears in a section title, so that it can be easily found.

Key *word Page*

access (to an international Treaty)	76
admissibility of a complaint	78
authority of a Committee (recognition of)	78
Charter od the United Nations	22
civil rights	32
Committee	76
communication	34
consultive status of an NGO	28
Convention	75
conventional mechanism	74
Covenant	75
Decision	40
Declaration	74
economic, social and cultural rights	32
fundamental freedoms	32
general recommendations	77
governmental organ	23
guarantees of a Treaty	75
human rights	32
international instruments	75
International Treaty	74
interpretative declaration (of an international Treaty)	76
mechanisms for implementation	75
NGO (non governmental organization)	28
periodic reports	77
permanent forum	42
political rights	32
procedure	33
promotion of human rights	33
protection of human rights	33
Protocol	75
ratification of an international instrument	76
reservations (to an international Treaty)	76
Resolution	40
right of veto	27

signing an international instrument	76
specialized agencies	23
specialized mechanism ("extra-conventional")	59
Special Rapporteur	34
State Party	75
subsidiary organs	23
suggestions	77
Treaty-monitoring bodies	76
United Nations system	23
Working Groups	34